# The Methodist Pulpit

## The Higher Ritualism

# The Higher Ritualism

Sermons preached in Independence Avenue Methodist
Episcopal Church, Kansas City, Missouri

*By*

## MATTHEW SIMPSON HUGHES, D. D.

OF THE SAINT LOUIS CONFERENCE.

CINCINNATI: JENNINGS AND GRAHAM
NEW YORK: EATON AND MAINS

# CONTENTS

| CHAPTER | | PAGE |
|---|---|---|
| I. | A DECLARATION OF INDEPENDENCE, | 9 |
| II. | THE RITUALISM OF OUR RELIGION, | 31 |
| III. | THE FELLOWSHIP OF CHRIST'S SUFFERINGS, | 55 |
| IV. | THE MISSION OF THE LITTLE CHILD, | 77 |
| V. | THE REMEMBRANCER, | 99 |
| VI. | HIGHER CRITICISM AND HUMAN DOCUMENTS, | 121 |
| VII. | THE FAILURES OF CHRISTIANITY, | 145 |
| VIII. | THE CORRELATION OF SPIRITUAL FORCES, | 168 |

# I.

## A DECLARATION OF INDEPENDENCE.

*"And John's disciples and the Pharisees were fast-*
*ing; and they came and said unto him: Why*
*do John's disciples and the disciples of the Phari-*
*sees fast, but Thy disciples fast not? And Jesus*
*said unto them: Can the sons of the bridecham-*
*ber fast, while the bridegroom is with them?*
*As long as they have the bridegroom with them,*
*they can not fast. But the days will come, when*
*the bridegroom shall be taken away from them,*
*and then they will fast in that day."*—Mark ii,
18-20. (R. V.)

THE events of record in this chapter mark the
dawn of religious liberty. The narrative contains
a declaration of independence on the part of Jesus,
and an emancipation proclamation on behalf of His
disciples. It is the beginning of the world's greatest religious revolution, and a prophecy of the final
deliverance of the sons of God from all burden-
some ritual and all priestly tyranny.

The religious forces of the time were crystallized, or crystallizing, about three centers. The first center was Tradition, with the scribes and Pharisees as its guardians. The second was Reformation, a movement led by John the Baptist, whose influence survived in the followers of the stern prophet of the wilderness. The third center, and least of all in point of numbers, was Revolution, represented by Jesus and His little circle. By their nature such diverse elements could not abide in peace. In fact, Jesus and His disciples had already departed from established customs in their manner of life. This non-conformity inflamed the partisan spirits of the old régime, gave opportunity to ready opposition, and inaugurated the "period of conflict" in our Lord's ministry. At the end of that conflict stood Calvary.

The occasions of the waxing antagonism of the religious leaders are not far to seek. The incidents of this chapter furnish us information by which we can interpret existing conditions. The grounds of complaint were three, at least, in number. There was, first, the extraordinary claims of Christ, who had forgiven sin when He healed the paralytic; there was His unconventional action in exalting Matthew, the tax-gatherer, to discipleship; and there was the revolutionary practice of our Lord and His disciples in the matters of fasting and Sabbath observance. As a result of these departures from accepted standards, His adversaries formulated three charges and urged them against Jesus— the charge of blasphemy, because He forgave sin; the charge of evil associations, based on His reception of Matthew and His social treatment of publicans and sinners; and the charge of non-conformity, growing out of the neglect of fasting and offenses against prescribed methods of Sabbath observance.

This passage, selected for our study, stands at the parting of the ways. The record is silent; but, no doubt, the incident described followed hot debates on subjects of belief and practice among the adherents of the three circles. Now appeal is made to the court of last resort. A judicial opinion is demanded and given. From this time forward the issue is joined. The conference of our text is but the preliminary skirmish of the long war for religious freedom. The questioners are "John's disciples and the Pharisees." A strange alliance! Religious controversy, as well as politics, makes strange bedfellows. These parties, so different in many respects, had this in common—they fasted.

They had this in common as against Jesus and His disciples—who did not fast. A superficial knowledge of human nature can easily account for the combination. The question was: "Why do John's disciples and the disciples of the Pharisees fast, but Thy disciples fast not?" The interview, as a whole, thus brings to our notice a question, an answer, and some general principles, and these we shall consider in turn.

It is obvious that the importance of the question to the minds of the delegation was in exact proportion to the value ascribed to fasting as a religious exercise among the Jews of the day. This would be true for the same reason that a sermon on "The Stations of the Holy Cross," or a study of "The Place of the Rosary in the Devotional Life," would make no appeal to a Protestant congregation. We make no use of these inventions in our system of religious culture. On the other hand, these mechanical appliances come to be regarded as integral parts of the life and practice of a devout Roman Catholic, and, therefore, any statement about them possesses for him an interest foreign to the Protestant mind. It is clear that the question and answer about fasting can not be appreciated at their full significance, unless the student of the pas-

sage knows something of the vital functions ascribed to this piece of religiosity in the formal religion of the period.

It may be true, as we are told, that fasting has in
all ages and among all peoples been practiced in
times of mourning, sorrow, and affliction.  It may
also be true that a basis for the observance can be
found in human nature, which under such conditions suspends the cravings of hunger and refuses
food.  But all this only places in stronger contrast
the part accorded fasting in the ritual of Judaism.
It is certainly a fact, and a striking fact, that, in
the history of the Old Testament, no examples of
fasting occur before the time of Moses.  It is more
marvelous still, in view of subsequent developments,
that only one regulation as to fasting was handed
down by Moses.  "The feasts of the Lord" have
pre-eminence in the Levitical law.  In all the Jewish Church year there was only one day of fasting
and humiliation, and that was the great Atonement-
day.  Provision for that day of fasting is found in
the injunction:  "Howbeit on the tenth day of this
seventh month is the day of atonement; and ye
shall afflict your souls."  But over against this one
day of the year in the Jewish Church, the days of
rejoicing in the calendar shone like stars in the sky.

But, in spite of the qualified sanction given to
fasting by Moses in the law, it had become a characteristic and commanding element in the Jewish
ritual. The exaggerated development of the practice had its origin during the captivity. During
that period of humiliation the Jews established four
annual fasts, to be observed in the fourth, fifth,
seventh, and tenth months. According to Jewish
authorities these new fasts commemorated historical calamities—such as the making of the golden
calf, the decree that those who came out of Egypt
should not enter Canaan, the destruction of the
temple by Nebuchadnezzar, and similar mournful
events. There was also the fast of Esther, kept in
memory of the original, ordered by Esther when
slaughter threatened all the Jews of the Persian
dominions. The number of annual fasts was gradually increased until they reached a total of no less
than twenty-eight. Then, in addition to these stated
seasons, occasional public fasts were proclaimed to
express national humiliation on account of sin and
disaster, to supplicate divine favor in behalf of some
great enterprise, or to seek divine protection against
some threatened danger.

There was more to follow. Not only had the
Jews multiplied annual and occasional fasts, but

there had also grown up an elaborate system of private fasts as a regular part of the current religious worship. The traditional code of the rabbis prescribed fasting twice in the week. The Pharisees in our Lord's time observed these biweekly fasts. They fasted on Thursday, because on that day Moses ascended Mount Sinai; and on Monday, because on that day he returned to the camp. This was the boast of the Pharisee in the parable, when he prayed: "I fast twice in the week." These private and voluntary fasts were frequently carried to extreme lengths. Indeed, it is recorded of a specially famous doctor that his face was always black with fasting. In brief, rabbinism magnified fasting until it became a species of slavery, a bondage too heavy to be borne.

But this is not all; nor is it the worst. The weight of superstition had been added to the physical burden. Spiritual and even magical powers were ascribed to fasting. It was associated with prayer, or, with prayer and almsgiving, as a condition of pardon of sins. It was a fond imagination that fasting as self-punishment and mortification would avert the anger of God. It was deemed the readiest means of turning aside drought, or pestilence, or national calamity. Extraordinary instances of its efficacy are related in Jewish legend. Of one Jewish saint it is declared that, by fasting, he was rendered proof against the fires of Gehenna, of which a realistic demonstration was given when his body was rendered proof against ordinary fire. To this sad recital it must be added, that the Jew fasted to secure lucky dreams, to obtain interpretations of dreams, to avert the evil import of dreams, or to acquire something eagerly desired. Let it be borne in mind that all this monstrous machinery for the physical treatment of souls had for the foundation of its legality the incident of the solemn day of expiation, found in the words: "On the tenth day of this seventh month . . . ye shall afflict your souls."

This survey gives us a conception of the interests involved, when those who were obedient to all these minute and multiplied requirements as to fasting came to Jesus and questioned: "Why do John's disciples and the disciples of the Pharisees fast, but Thy disciples fast not?"

All this is curious enough as ancient Church history, but it must be confessed that fasting is still a living subject, and that the teaching of Jesus in this passage is vital and practical for our own Christian time. For the twentieth century of our Lord's era finds us surrounded by disciples, not of John the Baptist, nor yet of the sect of the Pharisees, but of Christ, who have fasts innumerable, prescribed by canon law, and enforced by spiritual penalties.    Of great sections of the present-day Church, the question could not now be asked the Master: "Why do not Thy disciples fast?"  They do fast.  History has repeated itself.  The same influences that transformed Judaism from a religion of feasts into a cult of fasting have survived in the Christian Church and have accomplished their characteristic work.  The results are manifest.  The teachings of Jesus on the subject have been ignored; the calendar of the Church year has been defaced; and the genius of our religion has been misrepresented to the world.  The processes by which this state of things has been accomplished are more or less clearly marked in the history of the Christian centuries—they can only be suggested here.

"The Son of man came eating and drinking," that is, He was not an ascetic in His own habits of life, as was His herald, John.  In keeping with His own example, let it be emphasized as a starting-point, that our Lord wholly abstained from appointing any fast whatever as a part of His religion. Let it further be noticed, that, while recognizing the

2

fitness of fasting under appropriate conditions, the New Testament never makes fasting, of itself, a means of grace. And yet fasting appeared, with other Jewish relics and with Jewish estimates of value, in the Christian Church. At first it was purely voluntary and without superstition, but many influences combined to endow it with an exaggerated importance and to erect it into a permanent institution. The time came in the Christian, as in the Jewish Church, when fasts were regarded not only as aids, but as substitutes for the inner life; when they were considered as effectual in securing the forgiveness of sins.

By the sixth century, the historian informs us, fasting ceased to be a voluntary exercise. A council then decreed that any one neglecting to observe the stated times of abstinence should be treated as an offender against the laws of the Church. From this, it was only a step to the position of the eighth century, when fasting was extolled as meritorious, and disobedience of the laws of fasting was punished by excommunication. Later, we have accounts of how those who ate flesh during prescribed seasons of abstinence were visited with physical penalties, such as the loss of their teeth—a severity, however, later discontinued. Nor, after this, are we surprised to find that some of the old Jewish fasts were Christianized and given a place in the Church year. The four annual fasts of the Jews were thus introduced, deprived, however, of their specific Jewish character, by being assigned one to each of the four seasons. The Pharisee's "twice-a-week" fast was also adopted in the Christian Church; but Monday and Thursday were changed to Wednesday and Friday, because on Wednesday our Lord was betrayed and on Friday He was crucified.

Beyond this revival in Church practice, it was attempted to import the abomination of fasting under law into the spiritual teaching of Jesus. Ascetics—Pharisees of the new dispensation—inserted commandments to fast in the New Testament Scriptures. These interpolations are found in the Gospels, in the Acts of the Apostles, and in the Epistles. In the Gospel according to Matthew,* Jesus was made to say, in explanation of the disciples' failure to exorcise the evil spirit, when they came down from the mount of transfiguration: "Howbeit this kind goeth not out but by prayer and fasting." The Apostle Paul, champion of Christian liberty, was made to enjoin fasting with prayer, the old

---

* Matt. xvii, 21.

Jewish formula, in his first letter to the Corinthians. The student will notice that these interpolations, subversive of the essential spirit of Christianity, have been omitted in the Revised Version of the New Testament as glosses upon the original text.

But while the revisers have dropped the words from the text, the thing abides in the law of the Church and the practice of its members. In the Roman Catholic Church the times and character of fasts are prescribed by law. Fasting is numbered with the "satisfactory" work of "penance" together with prayer and almsgiving. Breaking the fasts commanded is reckoned with such sins as drunkenness, swearing, and debauchery. The great annual fast of the modern calendar is that of Lent, covering the forty days before Easter. When first introduced, Lent lasted but forty hours. In the eighth century its duration was extended to thirty-six days. Later still, it was lengthened to forty days. And what shall we more say? For time would fail us to speak of the fasts of the Ember-days, the vigils of Whitsuntide, of the Assumption of the Blessed Virgin Mary, of All Saints, the Rogation-days, and the whole long catalogue. Nor can we enter into the subject of the observance, with modifications and eliminations, by such bodies of Christians as those

of the Greek Church, the Church of England, the
Lutherans, and others. The point to be emphasized,
as sufficient for our purpose, is not simply that
these sects practice fasting, but that they enjoin it
at stated times by canon law, and enforce obedience
by penalty.

We are ready now to consider the way in which
Jesus met the challenge of His interviewers. The
direct question as to why His disciples did not fast
received a specific answer. He might effectively
have retorted in a different way. He could have
made His appeal to the law, pointing out the fact
that the frequent fasts observed by the Pharisees
and the disciples of John, were foreign to the law
of Moses and, therefore, without the warrant of authority. He could have sternly rebuked, as He did
under other circumstances, the vulgar hypocrisy
that characterized the dreary program of fasting
practiced by his hearers. He could have quoted the
ancient prophets to show that His questioners mis-
understood the essential nature of a fast: "Is not
this the fast that I have chosen? To loose the bands
of wickedness, to undo the heavy burdens, and to
let the oppressed go free, and that ye break every
yoke? Is it not to deal thy bread to the hungry,
and that thou bring the poor that are cast out to thy

house? When thou seest the naked, that thou cover him; and that thou hide not thyself from thine own flesh?" But the matter in hand received more thorough and satisfactory treatment. Without provoking any controversy as to the fasts of others, He explains why, under existing conditions, the Jesus-circle does not fast.

"And Jesus said unto them, can the sons of the bridechamber fast, while the bridegroom is with them? As long as they have the bridegroom with them they can not fast." In these words we have the first part of our Lord's explanation as to why His disciples are exempt from fasting. The effectiveness of the answer lies in the metaphor used. To appreciate its force we need only to remember the associations that the terms, "bridegroom" and "sons of the bridechamber" would find in the Jewish mind. They would suggest, first of all, the familiar scenes of the wedding festivities of the people. The metaphor would recall to them the nuptial ceremonies; the bride, veiled and crowned with myrtle, being taken to the house of the bridegroom; the wedding procession, passing through the streets at night, gay with festive dress, flaming with torchlights, enlivened with music, and greeted with song, as a religious duty, by all passersby. It would suggest to them the prolonged celebration of the "marriage feast," the rejoicings lasting for a week, with feasting, music, and dancing. It would remind them that, by universal consent and according to rabbinical law, this was to be a time of unmixed joy; that during the marriage-week all mourning was to cease and even the obligation of the prescribed daily prayers was to be suspended; and that it devolved upon all, as a religious responsibility, to cheer the hearts of the bride and bridegroom.

But the metaphor would carry a higher significance to Jewish thought. In the use of the figure of the bridegroom our Lord appropriated to Himself the rich imagery of the Old Testament Scriptures. The union of Jehovah and Israel was represented as a marriage. The Tabernacle and Temple, where Jehovah manifested Himself to His people, were designated as "the bridal chambers." The word would bring to the minds of those who heard, the associations of a whole circle of religious ideas, familiar to them since childhood. It was a claim that the Messiah had come; that, in the One who was speaking, the age-long national hope was at last realized; that in Him Jehovah had performed the mercy promised to the fathers and had remembered His holy covenant. And, especially, would

the use of the figure remind the disciples of John,
how, in their Master's last testimony to Jesus, he
had used the same title: "Ye yourselves bear me
witness, that I said, I am not the Christ, but that I
am sent before Him. He that hath the bride is the
bridegroom; but the friend of the bridegroom that
standeth and heareth him, rejoiceth greatly because
of the bridegroom's voice; this my joy is therefore
fulfilled."*

This, then, is the beautiful teaching contained
in the Master's utterance: Jesus is the Bridegroom,
long awaited and gladly welcomed; His disciples,
then and now, are "sons of the bride-chamber;"
while He is with them His presence disperses their
gloom. "They can not fast." This is said, of
course, not of the outward act, the abstaining from
food, which is possible at any time; but of fasting
as the expression of a sorrowful state of mind, the
only condition in which it can be reckoned as a
religious act. For fasting is synonymous with
mourning; it is the outward symbol of inward grief.
Where there is no sorrow, fasting is hypocrisy. All
this is in harmony with the Gospel idea of blessed-
ness in Christ. With the presence of the Savior,
"sorrow and sighing shall flee away." His coming

---

*John iii, 28, 29.

into the life creates the distinctive state of mind which characterizes Christianity as an experience. That distinctive state of mind is joy, and while joy rings wedding bells in the heart, sincerity demands that no signals of sorrow shall be displayed.

"But the day will come," continued Jesus with His instruction, "when the bridegroom shall be taken away from them, and then they will fast in that day." These words are memorable as being the first intimation of the goal towards which Jesus had thus early set His face. A dim hint ("even so must the Son of man be lifted up") had been given privately to Nicodemus. But the phrase "taken away" occurs nowhere else in the New Testament, and clearly suggests a violent end. The future is stored with sorrow for the disciples who now rejoice in the Bridegroom's companionship. The words are chill with the premonition of coming death.

"They will fast in that day." We may not agree with interpreters who, like Neander, hold that this passage is simply an intimation of the approach of a period of general mourning, in which the term "fast" has a derivative meaning, signifying mental affliction rather than physical denial. But clearly the words "will fast" are not imperative, but prophetic; they do not give a command, they state a fact. When the time of sorrow comes the fasts of the disciples will be voluntary, and not compulsory; they will spring from a feeling of the heart and not from the authority of an order. It is not an intimation that the Pharisees will be able to bend the disciples of Jesus to their will as concerning fasting in that day; but that no prescription will be needed, because they will fast as the natural expression of sorrow. And we must wholly dissent from the Roman Catholic inference based upon these words—that since the death of Christ it becomes a Christian duty to fast. That is to affirm that we have only an absent Christ. That is to make the phrase "taken away" cover all the space between the Ascension and the Second Advent. That is to ignore the fact that the Scriptures do not countenance the notion that the Ascension robbed the disciples of Christ either of privilege or of joy. That is to forget that He said: "Lo, I am with you alway, even unto the end of the world." That is to overlook the circumstance that a consistent course of action, based on such an interpretation, would suggest abstinence from food during the entire year—a fatal objection, in more senses than one.

But the study is not to be closed until we point out the principles contained in the teaching, and show the boundless sweep of their possible application. For there was involved in this passage at arms, not simply the matter of fasting, but, beyond that, the Christian's relation to all the perplexing and practical problems of ritual observance. To a limited question we have an unlimited answer. The inquiry was born of the moment and its antagonisms; but Jesus foresaw the criticism that would challenge His kingdom at each forward step. So He enlarged His words to cover the centuries. The whole subject of external forms is covered by principles more exhaustive than volumes of discussion, because applicable to any possible case that can arise in the future. As in geometry the complex theorems about cones, pyramids, and spheres are based upon the principles of the science as set forth in its axioms; as in the Constitution of the United States we have the principles of government upon which all State and national legislation must be based; so in this teaching of our Lord upon the subject of fasting we find the fundamental and organic laws by which we may ever govern our relations to religious forms, rites, ceremonies and observances.

From the data before us, at least three laws of Christian ritualism emerge. There is, first of all, the law of sincerity. It is fundamental in Christianity that every outward manifestation must be the expression of an inward state. Our observances must possess the qualities of spirit and of truth. "Be not as the hypocrites." The theatrical in religion has its only reward in being seen of men. When joy gladdens the heart do not attempt the sad countenance. When the Bridegroom is with you do not hang out the symbols of mourning because alleged authority has issued a decree of fasting. Such conduct is forced and unreal, and, therefore, unchristian. We are also under the law of liberty. Fasting is not commanded and it is not forbidden. In this matter, the Christian is a free man. He must "seek first the kingdom of God and his righteousness," and if fasting becomes an essential means to that end, well and good. The disciple of Christ will use that which he finds most helpful in his spiritual development. He will make use of fasting or any other form, not as a mechanical observance of a prescribed regimen, but as a voluntary means to a devoutly desired end. We will also observe the law of congruity. This lesson is conveyed in the second illustration given by the Master on the general subject—that of the new patch on the old garment. Fasting is not a matter of prescription, but of fitness. If the canon law of your Church calls you to mourning at a set time, that time may find your heart rejoicing in the Lord, and the exercise would be as inappropriate as merriment at a funeral or tears at a jubilee. "Let no man therefore judge you in meat, or in drink, or in respect of a feast day, or a new moon, or a Sabbath-day."*

The message is for each individual Christian. We have our joyous seasons because of the conscious presence and favor of our Lord. For the loyal heart with a present Christ an observance that is the expression of mourning is out of the question. Joy is the characteristic product of a vital religious experience. Is the Bridegroom with you? Then rejoice and let your soul delight itself in the Lord. You have heard glad tidings of great joy—do not weep! You have peace with God—do not afflict your soul! You sit in "the heavenly places in Christ"—do not affect sackcloth and ashes! Christ abides with you—lift the flag of joy in token of His presence. As long as you have the Bridegroom you can not fast.

But when the Bridegroom is taken away; when

*Col. ii, 16.

sin separates the heart from Christ; and when the supreme blessing of intercourse with the Beloved is interrupted; then comes the true call to fasting. The exercise will then be no petty abstinence, recommended as to time, length, and incidents, by some ecclesiastical authority; but it will be a great, black sorrow finding a natural and appropriate expression. The bereaved soul will proclaim its own fast; the stricken heart will be its own calendar; sorrow, and not the clock, will strike the hour of observance. Such fasting, a symbol of the heart's desire, shall be as a sacrament in the sight of heaven, and such mourning shall be blessed, for it shall be comforted.

## II.

## THE RITUALISM OF OUR RELIGION.

*"Pure religion and undefiled before God and the
Father is this, To visit the fatherless and widows
in their affliction, and to keep himself unspotted
from the world."*—James i, 27.

THE interpretation of the text hinges on the
word "religion." This fact does not simplify our
task. Like many of our great and familiar terms
it is not easy to define. Religion is many-sided. It
presents itself to the mind in many aspects. Our
English translation carries with it an idea foreign
to the intention of the "apostle of common sense."
The use of the word "religion" in the aspect here
set forth, persists in the dictionary, but is obsolete
in common usage.

The word "religion" is, in the original, more
nearly synonymous with the term ritualism. Alford renders it "religious worship, especially that
which consists in ceremonies." Trench says it is
"predominantly the ceremonial service of religion."

While Dr. Hatch thus sums up the results of his investigation: "Religion in its external aspect, as worship or as one mode contrasted with another, must be held to be its meaning in the New Testament as in contemporary writers." It is not a definition of the essence of Christianity, but a description of its external manifestations. Religion, in the sense of the text, is the fruit of which piety is the root; the body of which godliness is the soul; the language of which the Spirit of Christ is the thought; the garment in which the Christian life arrays itself. It is related to vital Christianity as light to the sun, fragrance to the flower, and smoke to sacrificial worship. It describes the cultus of Christianity—the visible part of religious service. It is an outward sign of the inward grace. It is as though James said: "Instead of rites and ceremonies (lustrations, sacrifices, fastings, circumcisions, feasts, and other observances), such as characterize other religions, let it be known that the pure and undefiled ritualism, approved of God our Father, is something higher and nobler, for it consists in purity of life and deeds of helpfulness."

Equally decisive as to the meaning of the passage is the evidence as to the use of the term three hundred years ago, when it first found a place in the

Authorized Version. A living language is constantly changing. Wycliffe's Bible is like Greek for the reader of to-day, and Chaucer's English is difficult for the modern student. Archbishop Trench has an interesting discussion on the subject in his "New Testament Synonyms." He shows that the word religion was then identified with ceremonial worship. Speaking of the passage under consideration he declares that the author's intention is obscured to the English reader because the terms "religious" and "religion" "possessed a meaning once which they now possess no longer, and in that meaning are here employed." He notes the old meaning given to the word by Milton in "Paradise Lost," where he characterizes heathen idolatries as being

"adorned
With gay *religions* full of pomp and gold."

He also notes the frequent use of the term in like sense in the "Homilies." All this is vitally important. To us religion means godliness. It stands, in common usage, for the sum total of Christianity. But in King James's time it was limited in its sense to the external aspect of religion. It can readily be seen that the lost meaning of the word might entail serious consequences.

3

With this definition the passage is found to be in accord with the spirit of the Epistle. The instruction throughout is practical in its character. Its essence is found in the preceding words: "But be ye doers of the Word, and not hearers only." It is noteworthy that James, the representative of Christian Judaism, nowhere in this Epistle touches upon the subject of the ceremonial law. He is only interested to detail the practical way in which those begotten of the Word of Truth are to exhibit the new life to the world. Those who are "the first-fruits of His creatures" are to manifest the life in their characters as individuals and in their social intercourse as members of the Christian fraternity. In this will be found obedience to the law. Without this governing spirit, as he emphatically declares in the preceding verse, the most zealous devotion to ritual forms is useless—"this man's religion is vain." The teaching then rises to its climax in the declaration that the ritualism of the Christ-life consists in the elements of character and conduct upon which he lays stress. The passage with its general principles is the Epistle in miniature.

A striking confirmation of this, as the true and primitive conception of the external aspects of Christianity, is found in the early pages of Church history. This feature is nowhere better stated than by Principal Fairbairn, in "The Place of Christ in Modern Theology." Describing the distinctive characteristics of the new religion, he says: "It stood among the ancient faiths as a strange and extraordinary thing—a priestless religion, without the symbols, sacrifices, ceremonies, officials hitherto, save by prophetic Hebraism, held to be the religious all in all." In another place he speaks of the beginnings of Christianity and the first sentences are a paraphrase of James's teaching. "Men are God's sons; filial love is their primary duty, fraternal love their common and equal obligation. Worship does not depend on sacred persons, places, or rites; but is a thing of spirit and truth. The best prayer is secret and personal; the man who best pleases God is not the scrupulous Pharisee, but the penitent publican. Measured by the standard of a sacerdotal religion, Jesus was not a pious man. He spoke no word, did no act, that implied the necessity of an official priesthood for His people. He enforced no sacerdotal observance, instituted no sacerdotal order, promulgated no sacerdotal law. . . . It has no temple, save the living man; no sacrifices, save those of the spirit and the life; no sensuous sanctities." Indeed, so devoid was early Christianity of anything like ritualism, that Mosheim gives as one reason for its introduction, which began in the second century, a desire on the part of the Church to rebut the charge of atheism made against Christians because they had none of the external paraphernalia of religion.

The genuine Christian ritual, then, is not that which has been invented by men, promulgated by councils, enforced by canon law, or hallowed by use and age. But we have an authoritative ritual which bears a threefold commendation: it is pure; it is undefiled; and it is approved of God. The word "pure" is positive in its content, designating the essential nature of the ritualism. The term "undefiled" stands for its negative purity. It is free from any contamination resulting from contact with external things, such as the associations of pagan idolatries or the corruptions of Christian doctrines. "Before God" means that this is the ritualism with the divine approval. "Before the face" was a well-known Hebraism conveying the idea of acceptance on the part of the one thus showing favor. The man who stands before God is a man accepted of God. A ritualism, pure and undefiled before God, is one that bears the seal of His approval. Here is something higher than man's invention; here is

something better than an article borrowed from the
Egyptians.

There is a beautiful touch in the passage likely
to be overlooked. This ritualism is approved of
God as "Father." It is the inspiration of the divine
love and compassion. God, in His most intimate
and personal relation to His people, expressed in
the Christ-given name of Father, gives the creden-
tial of His approbation to this ritual manifestation
of the life which is His gift. As holy, the Father
wills that men shall be "partakers of the divine nature." As loving, the Father wills that the sons of
God shall serve those of the universal family who
are in need and affliction. The true ritualism has
its source in the Divine Fatherhood.

Of the two distinctive elements in the Christian
ritual the first mentioned is *beneficence*. This is expressed in a characteristic Hebrew way—"to visit
the fatherless and the widows in their affliction."
The writer uses what the rhetoricians call synec-
doche—a figure in which a part is made to designate the whole. We make free use of the form in
common speech. Thus laborers are known as
"hands;" a fleet of ships as so many "sail;" the
home is spoken of as a "fireside" or a "hearthstone."
Here the writer uses a concrete example for the

comprehensive duty. Selecting a class peculiarly
helpless in Oriental lands, as everywhere else—a
class proverbially representative of the needy and
afflicted—he presents the widows and orphans as
typical of all sorts and conditions of men in need of
sympathy and succor. One of the liturgical rites,
appropriately symbolizing our faith and worthily
uttering our worship to God, is help for need and
sympathy for distress. Beneficence is a practical
manifestation of godliness. Charity may be a genuine expression of piety. The Spirit of Christ is a
spirit of benevolence; the ministry of Christ is a
ministry of beneficence. Therefore the natural and
fitting expression of the Christ-spirit in the heart
will be found in the imitation of His beneficence in
the life. In no other form can the mind of Christ
towards others be so truthfully uttered. Beneficence will be, of necessity, the genuine, spontaneous
outflow of a spirit-filled life. This truth has found
utterance in the lines of the Quaker poet:

> "He serves thee best who loveth most
>   His brothers and thine own.
> Thy litanies, sweet offices
>   Of love and gratitude;
> Thy sacramental liturgies,
>   The joy of doing good."

This rite can not be performed by proxy. The prayer-wheel may be placed where willing waters will turn it while the worshiper sleeps; the congregation may sit in listless mood while minister or priest "conducts the service;" contributions, more or less liberal, may put agents into contact with need and distress; but here the personal element is emphasized. A man can no more turn this part of the Christian ritual over to personal representatives than he can salary another to attend prayer-meetings in his behalf or celebrate the Lord's Supper for his spiritual benefit. "Official charity," born of the pervading spirit of Christianity, does not always preserve enough of its original inspiration to save it from disrepute. This ritual provides for the symbolism of individual action. It directs personal contact with human woe and want. The liturgy reads: "To visit" the afflicted; and "to visit" them in their affliction.

Organized charity aims to provide what we call "the necessities of life." In this category we include food, shelter, clothing, fuel, and medicine. But the afflicted need the personal touch as well as the material relief. Interest, sympathy, and friendship must be reckoned among "the necessities of life." The minds and the hearts of the world's unfortunates have their thirsts and hungers, and these can not be satisfied by impersonal and professional care for their bodies. The word of cheer may be more efficacious than the second-hand coat; the assurance of friendly interest may be more welcome than the ton of coal; human sympathy in time of affliction may be more blessed than the prescription of the free dispensary. Our own experiences help us to understand the cry of the aged recipient of charity: "I do n't want things, I want folks." The superiority of this personal help in contrast with proxy methods is well stated by Mr. Lecky, in his "European Morals," in these luminous sentences: "The rich man, prodigal of money, which to him is of little value, but altogether incapable of any personal attention to the object of his alms, often injures society by his donations; but this is rarely the case with that far nobler charity which makes men familiar with the haunts of wretchedness, and follows the object of his care through all the phases of his life."

We are not to imagine that this provision for personal contact is altogether in the interest of the poor and afflicted. There is a reaction of blessing for the visitor. This rite, as all others ought to be, is intended to be a means of grace. There is a certain warmth for the heart in writing a check from

charitable motives; but there is an overflowing
blessing in personal ministry. Personal aid for the
afflicted is not only an evidence of piety—it also
nourishes and strengthens the higher life. Here,
as elsewhere, exercise promotes health and strength.
This is a direction in the interest of the well and
strong and comfortable, as really as it is a provision
for the afflicted. Lowell, with a poet's insight, saw
this truth and left it with us in "The Vision of Sir
Launfal." He makes the Christ speak to the pil-
grim knight who has just shared his water and
crust with the roadside leper "for Christ's sweet
sake:"

> "Not what we give, but what we share,—
> For the gift without the giver is bare;
> Who gives himself with his alms feeds three—
> Himself, his hungering neighbor, and me."

In addition to beneficence, the second essential
element of this approved ritualism is cleanness of
life. This is put in a characteristic way: "And to
keep himself unspotted from the world." The liturgical color in our ritual is white. The figure is suggested by the Jewish ceremonial law. The idea of
holiness was imparted to the Hebrews by the kindergarten method; that is, in object lessons. The
presence of the abstract term in our vocabulary is

due to a long and complicated educational process. The absolute necessity of purity in man's conception of God and in the life of the individual is the basis of the Levitical ritual. The division of the Palestine animals into clean and unclean; the selection for sacrifice from the clean animals of one without spot or blemish; the setting aside of a special class to make the offering; the purification of priest and sacrifice as essential to the act of worship; the repeated purifyings of the camp and the people,—all served to form the notion, first of physical, and then of moral purity in the minds of the people. The fine gold of the great idea was then coined into the terms now current in the Christian world. The Jew was polluted by coming into contact with many things of the external world. A grave, a corpse, an unclean animal, or a fellow ceremonially defiled imparted contamination, and a cleansing process was necessary before he could participate in the service of the Temple or associate with his co-religionists. How natural, then, for a Hebrew to speak of a clean life as one "unspotted from the world!"

This part of the Christian ritual, like beneficence, really deserves the shop-worn panegyric, "a beautiful and impressive service." It is the natural outcome of a religion with a righteous God, a sinless

Christ, and a Holy Spirit. What else could be expected of an evangel whose burden is salvation from sin? What ceremonial could be more appropriate for a process of redemption begun in regeneration and continued in sanctification, each stage of development bringing nearer the cheering assurance, "We shall be like Him?" The work of the Holy Spirit in the heart is guaranteed to manifest itself in the outward life. The world has taken knowledge of the fact. The author of "The Varieties of Religious Experience," opens a section of one of his lectures with these words: "The next religious symptom which I will note is what I have called Purity of Life." Studying the religious life as an investigator, the eminent psychologist has noted the fact that one of the features of religious experience is a sacrificial desire to get rid of everything deemed unworthy of the object of worship. The disciple of the Holy One not only learns to do good, he also departs from evil. A blameless life is an essential element in the cultus exterior of Christianity. The energies expended in this endeavor are given to the noble ritual service of our religion. The man who thus believes and practices is the highest Churchman.

Let it also be emphasized that what God hath

joined together in this approved ritual, man must not put asunder. Two halves make this whole. Christian ritualism has two essentials—beneficence and holiness; not separated, but one and indivisible; not in themselves simply, but jointly, a manifestation of the new life. Neither, by itself, is an adequate expression. There are those who would give assiduous performance to the one, and persistent neglect to the other. Men practice charity who make no claim to purity; men gather wealth by questionable methods who hope by generous gifts to secure approbation, human and divine; men with soiled hands exalt charity into a religion, and hope that generosity will offset their vices. But it is not benevolence *or* holiness, but benevolence *and* holiness. "Unspotted from the world" must be linked with the visiting of the fatherless and widows in their affliction. Others there are whose theory is comprehended in purity, but who find small place in their system for beneficence. They are enthusiastic believers, perhaps, in entire sanctification; they may be vociferous professors of holiness; they can expatiate upon the subject of heart-purity and deliverance even from "inbred sin;" but when it comes to personal ministries or organized philanthropies they are minus quantities. For such let it be urged that

both beneficence and purity belong to the fruit of
the Spirit. Vital Christianity is not an experience
divorced from service, nor is charity in deed a substitute for godliness in character. The two must
stand hand in hand at God's altar of life. Either,
without the other, is only a caricature and not a
faithful representation of the religion of Jesus
Christ.

The first thing that impresses us as we grasp
this Christian conception of ritualism, is its ac-
cordance with the genius of the whole Bible. Even
in the Old Testament, a literature born of a religion
essentially liturgical in its character, you will find
the same teaching. Samuel declared that "to obey
is better than sacrifice." The evangelical prophet,
Isaiah, made his protest against a false reliance upon
rites and ceremonies. He denounced the whole external system of religion in the absence of a holy
life and a practical benevolence. He went so far as
to declare that conformity to the ceremonial law,
without these essential elements, was no better than
the abominations of heathen idolatry, with its human victims and its unclean offerings: "He that
killeth an ox is as if he slew a man; he that sacri-
ficeth a lamb, as if he cut off a dog's neck; he that
offereth an oblation, as if he offered swines' blood;

he that burneth incense, as if he blessed an idol."
Micah asks the question: "Wherewithal shall I
come before the Lord, and bow myself before the
high God?" He asks if God will be pleased with
burnt offerings, calves of a year old, thousands of
rams, ten thousand rivers of oil, or even with the
sacrifice of the first-born for the father's transgres-
sions? The conclusion is the same as that given by
James in the text. The costly sacrifice, the gor-
geous ceremonial, amount to nothing in God's sight
in the absence of beneficence and purity. "He hath
showed thee, O man, what is good; and what doth
the Lord require of thee, but to do justly, and to
love mercy, and to walk humbly with thy God."
The Psalms are so free from any other ritualism
that they supply expression for the high religious
experiences of those who know little of the ancient
temple and its liturgy. And what of the New Testament? There you will find such an absence of
material symbolism that Paul speaks of our religion
as "the ministration of the Spirit." Trying to con-
dense Christian obligations into two terms, no better could be found than these—purity and philanthropy.

We are further impressed with the fact that
these ritual forms are worthy symbols of the Christ-

life. Sinlessness and service were the characteristics of our Lord's life, and those who represent
Him can find no better media than holiness and
helpfulness. We turn with a sigh of profound relief to the divinely approved ritualism after listening to the puerilities of modern ritualistic discussion. We can not forbear comparisons, even with
knowledge of their odious character. The "two
points" of James are infinitely beyond the "six
points" of the Anglo-Catholics—the eastward position in celebrating, the mixed chalice, the altar
lights, eucharistic vestments, wafer bread, and incense. The white life of the Christian is incom-
parably superior to what the ritualists call the "liturgical colors." Compare the conception of the
text with a seriously intended statement such as
this: "I accept only the five revealed colors, viz.,
red, white, yellow, blue, and purple,—and protest
against the use of black, green, brown, and other
fancy colors in the services of the Church." The
deed of beneficence is of transcendent value in com-
parison with the rite of the sign of the cross, the
genuflections of formal worship, or even the pros-
trations of stated adorations. The religion of Jesus
Christ can not be adequately symbolized by a re-
version to the kindergarten methods of the child-

hood of Judaism, as some sects of our time seem to imagine. The real object lessons of Christianity, spelling out its essential nature to the world at large, will be found in the white robes of personal purity and the open hands of Christly benevolence.

The subject also impresses us as timely. Not that our communion is in especial danger of excessive ritualism. Few show symptoms of having been inoculated to any degree with the toxin of the liturgical mania of the last fifty years. But it is timely because fundamentals are always in order. The insistence upon the authoritative way in which Christianity is to be presented to the world in its external aspects, leads us into no quarrel with the simple rites and dignified conduct of public worship conducive to decency and order. We do not forget that the ritual serves to impart and preserve the historic truths of Christianity, and that they may witness to doctrinal truths as well. We have not overlooked the fact that Christ established two simple rites—baptism and the Lord's Supper; the first bearing perpetual witness to the doctrine of cleansing from sin, and the second a monument to the historical fact that Christ died for our sins. We do not ignore the inference that, as externals have their place in the divine economy, the absence of anything like liturgical forms in the New Testament leaves their use to the godly judgment of the worshiper.  We should heed the demand of refined taste as well as the satisfaction of devout impulse in the offices of public worship.  But, because all these things are weak through the flesh, we need to be constantly kept in touch with the vital and essential in our religion.

One of our common errors has to do with the function of ritualism.  Usually its value is estimated on the basis of what it will accomplish in the spiritual improvement of the worshiper.  But the New Testament conception, both in our text and elsewhere, indicates that the function of a rite is expression rather than inspiration.  This is true of baptism.  We are baptized, not that we may secure that which the symbol signifies, but because we are supposed to be already in possession of that which is represented by the outward sign.  The symbol expresses the fact that the subject of baptism is at the time free from the guilt of sin.  This is true of the Lord's Supper.  As a Sacrament it gives expression to an allegiance already existent.  As a Eucharist it expresses a gratitude already in the heart.  As a Communion it is expressive of a double fellowship already enjoyed—a fellowship with Christ and a

4

fellowship with Christ's people. Almsgiving without the spirit of benevolence in the heart is an abomination in the sight of God. Prayer must always utter a sense of need and a recognition of dependence. It is not doubted that these observances, proceeding from a right spirit, have a reaction of blessing and thus become means of grace. But only to him that hath shall it be given. The form must first be vitalized; of itself it possesses no life-giving power. The spirit of the worshiper sanctifies the worship. The rite can not quicken the soul. The outward ceremony can not produce the spiritual reality; it can only bear witness to its existence. Water applied to the body does not cleanse the soul; bread and wine do not transform the character; the humble heart is not the product of the bended knee; benevolence is not related to beneficence as effect to cause. These and all ritual observances must first be expressions of the inner life. The attempt to vitalize religious experience by ceremonial machinery can only result in a sort of galvanic activity. The primary function of ritualism is the expression of life. Lacking the spirit, the form is but hypocrisy.

In the use of rites there is a progressive peril. There is, first, a tendency to confuse the symbol with the reality. Later the symbol is likely to be substituted for that which it represents. This has been the history even of the two simple rites established by Christ. Baptism symbolizes cleansing from sin, but we have the dogma of baptismal regeneration. The Lord's Supper symbolizes the shed blood and broken body of the Savior, but we have the doctrine of transubstantiation and the sacrifice of the Mass. Phillips Brooks told of an English clergyman whose sermon he heard on the occasion of the celebration of the fortieth anniversary of Queen Victoria's reign. The Church of England rector protested against the prevalent opinion that religion was on the decline in the kingdom, and the following was the reason given for the faith that was in him: "Whereas forty years ago the black gown was used in many pulpits, it was now almost never seen, but the surplice had taken its place; in the second place, that while formerly the choral service was considered the especial mark of a peculiar class, it was now almost universally used in English Churches." First confusion, and then substitution, is the natural history of ritualism as a disease. The ultimate effects are visible in the older communions. Frederick Robertson stated the case correctly when he said: "Romanists announce a salvation which is inseparable from ceremonial ob-

servances, and has so interblended and intermixed
ritual with ethics that it is next to impossible for an
ordinary mind to discriminate between them." The
fruit of such a system is typified in the Italian brig-
and kneeling in the Church to pray for success in
robbery or murder; or in the American assassins
who could take a life, but would not remove an amu-
let from the body when they stripped their victim.

When such conditions result, the external system must perish in the interest of the worshipers.
That is the lesson of an episode given us in the ancient Scriptures. The brazen serpent of the wilderness had been preserved as a memorial of the sin and
deliverance of Israel in the wilderness. But when
the reverence for the relic degenerated into superstition Hezekiah came to the rescue of the worshipers. He "broke in pieces the brazen serpent that
Moses had made; for to those days the children of
Israel did burn incense to it; and he called it
Nehushtan, that is, a piece of brass."

That is one of the lessons of the Jewish captivity,
as interpreted by Dean Stanley in his "History of
the Jewish Church." In one respect this captivity
was an emancipation. Torn away from all the external forms of temple worship, they developed a

species of religious liberty they had never known
before. The overthrow of the sanctuary on Mount
Zion inspired a deeper sense of the unseen than had
been produced by the elaborate ritual of the temple
service. Deprived of the sacrificial system of worship they were brought face to face with God. As
the author describes it: "Man's necessity is God's
opportunity; the loss of earthly ceremonial is the
occasion for heavenward aspirations. And hence
it is that from the Captivity dates, not indeed the
first use, but the continued and frequent use of
prayer . . . as the chief access to the Invisible
Divinity. Prayer now literally took the place of
their evening and morning sacrifice, their morning
and evening incense. Now for the first time we hear
of men 'kneeling upon their knees three times a day,'
praying and making supplication to God. Now for
the first time assemblies for prayer, and praise, and
lamentation, as afterwards in houses and syna-
gogues, were gathered by the watersides. . . .
And not in prayer only, but the homely acts of beneficence and kindness rose now for the first time to
the full dignity of religious ordinances." It was
also necessary, as the author avers, that there should
be a second overthrow of the Temple in the interest
of spiritual progress, coincident with the inaugura-

tion of the consummation of Judaism in the rise of Christianity.

But the ritualism approved of God possesses permanent elements. It will never wax old. It is as abiding as the purposes of God and as lasting as the needs of man. It will never be thrown upon the scrap-pile of the ages in the interest of a purer religion. It will continue until the whole world is a temple of God crowded with devout worshipers. It will persist until each common meal becomes a sacrament, because when men eat and drink it will be done "in the name of the Lord Jesus." It will flourish until the bells of the horses in the streets shall bear the inscription of the high priest's miter, "Holiness to the Lord." It will spread until all Christians understand that they belong to "a royal priesthood," and with holy hands offer sacrifices at the altars of daily life, acceptable to God by Jesus Christ. This is the simple and sublime ritualism of our religion. This we should study. This we should preach. This we should practice.

# III.

## THE FELLOWSHIP OF CHRIST'S SUF-FERING.

*"That I may know Him . . . and the fellow-ship of His sufferings."*—Phil. iii, 10.

THESE words voice an aspiration of the Apostle Paul. Let us frankly confess that we are not eager for the experience. Suffering, in all its kinds and degrees, is something from which we instinctively shrink. Instead of seeking it, we pray to be deliv-ered from it. The utterance, therefore, sounds like the voice of religious hysteria. It seems to reveal a positively unwholesome state of mind. The words awaken within us no answering enthusiasm. If they embody a Christian privilege, we do not care to claim it. At best we think such whole-hearted de-votion might characterize a few choice souls, but it does not strike us as an attainment for the average Christian. It is not the fellowship with Christ of which we habitually think. We seek the fellowship of His joy; we are ready to share the fellowship of His victories; we hope for the fellowship of His eternal glory; but "the fellowship of His sufferings" —that is another matter.

But making deductions for the fervor of the writer born of his unique experience; remembering that such declarations, like most of the great hymns of the Church, mark the high tides of the spirit and not the low ebbings of life; there is something to be said before we shelve the text as a mere outburst of religious ecstasy. The key to any problem involved lies in the simple fact that Paul loved his Lord. This chapter throbs with devotion to Christ. These words are words of love; this desire is the desire of love. It is a commonplace fact that love craves complete fellowship with its object. Even animal affection is in evidence here. The lioness of the desert and the tigress of the jungle suffer with their offspring. The parent chooses this fellowship with the child. Husband and wife find themselves drawn more closely together in the partnership of affliction. A satisfactory test of friendship is given by fellowship in sufferings. The one who deserts us in sorrow and trouble can not satisfy us by protested affection. This longing of a loving heart, so true to the nature of love as we mark its ordinary manifestations, can not be ignored on the ground that it is abnormal.

Preaching to a congregation of those who would answer with the disciple, "Yea, Lord, Thou knowest that I love Thee," the chosen subject is not out of place. We do not fear that it will give us a gloomy and forbidding view of the religious life. It may thus appear to those who mistake the nature of the Christian life. It will not appeal to those who are selfish, to those who are indolent, to those who are cowardly, to those who regard religion as a cheap and comfortable device for getting into heaven. But the call of the ambassador for Christ is not to be made to such motives. Appeals to selfishness will not people the kingdom of God. Success is not in such methods. Some one has said: "You can tempt a man to the pit with sweetmeats, but when he starts for heaven he wants to feel that he is a hero." Christ appealed to the highest in man. That in itself is an evidence of divinity. Those forms of religion that stoop to human standards; that demand no toil and sacrifice; that offer material inducement instead of heroic opportunity, have a sickly life and die a lingering death.

One might imagine that men would flock to the standards of ease and comfort in religion. History

bears witness to the contrary. Those sects and re-
ligionists most abused, most familiar with the fellowship of sufferings, have been the most successful.
The greater the difficulties, the sterner the circumstances, the harder the conditions, the more sturdy
and the more fruitful has been the religious movement. That is the memorable lesson of the triumph
of early Christianity. That is the teaching of history in regard to the beginning of every great religious movement. The Protestant Reformation, the
Religious Society of Friends, the Presbyterian
Church, the Baptist Church, early Methodism, and,
more recently, the Salvation Army, all came up out
of great tribulation. They made their appeal to the
heroic in human nature, and were not disappointed.
The easy thing, the pleasant thing, the selfish thing,
are perfectly consistent in the minds of men with
going to the devil. They can never be made the
motive forces of goodness and greatness. It is time
a great silence fell upon sugar-and-water coaxings
in the Christian Church. You can fill the Church
with milksops under such evangelism. Their presence may swell our pride of numbers, but it will
cripple our energies, dilute our principles, and hin-
der our true progress. We need rock-Christians in
these days of peace and plenty. The climate in

which we live is enervating. We are in danger of becoming religious lotus-eaters. There is special need of the enforcement of the heroic aspects of our faith, and to this category our subject belongs.

Approaching the positive lessons of our theme, let us pause to notice that there are some sufferings which, by their very nature, are excluded from this high fellowship. There are some sufferings we can not share with Christ; and some of our sufferings He can not share with us. The aspiration of Paul was futile if it sought a part in the atoning sufferings of Christ for the sin of the world. In this we can have no fellowship. The apostle recognized this fact. He asked the Corinthians: "Was Paul crucified for you? or were ye baptized in the name of Paul?" Recently there has been some very loose use of the sacred title, "Savior." We have heard it declared that all Christians are saviors. The term may, perhaps, be legitimately used in describing some functions of the disciples of Christ. But such use of the word must never lead to forgetfulness of the characteristic truth of our religion that there is only one sacrifice for sin; that there is only one Savior for the sinner; there is "only one name given under heaven and among men whereby we can be saved;" and that name is not yours, nor mine,

nor the name of the apostle. Christ is the propitia-
tion for our sins. He provided full redemption centuries before we were born. The fellowship of
those sufferings we can only know by enjoying the
blessings that they bestow. From any other fellowship in them all men are excluded.

Nor are the sufferings of the text those incident
to the fact that Christ was found in fashion as a
man. He participated in our common sufferings by
virtue of His humanity. But these are *our* sufferings, and not *His* sufferings. The passage evidently
refers to those sufferings which only a Christian
life can share with the Master. The ordinary afflic-
tions of life, which come both upon the just and the
unjust, are outside the limits of the text. Identity
of sufferings would not satisfy the desire. Christ
was poor; but men are poor and Christless. Christ
was persecuted; but men have been persecuted who
rejected Christ. Christ knew hunger; but men
have been hungry and godless. Christ was crucified; but one of the malefactors who was crucified
at the same time and place had no fellowship with
the Savior. The impenitent thief suffered with
Christ, but suffering, in itself, will create no such
fellowship as that of the prayer. This leaves out
of our consideration the sorrows common to man-

kind, and also the peculiar sufferings of Christ as
the Redeemer of men.

There are some of our sufferings that exclude
Christ from their fellowship. To some of our familiar experiences He was a stranger. *"His"* sufferings" says the text. The sorrows of committed sin
the Holy One never knew. In the endurance of the
personal consequences of sin no man may lay to
his soul the flattering unction that he is suffering
with Christ. The indictments of an accusing conscience, the shame that dogs the heels of the wrong-
doer, were no part of His experience. One of the
most remarkable features of the Gospel record is
its revelation of the self-consciousness of our Lord.
Not once in all its pages do we find a trace of the
consciousness of guilt. There is never an indication
of the penitence that becomes a heart alienated
from God. He never descended into the depths of
despair where the only relief is the sinner's cry for
mercy. Throughout His whole white life He could
look full and fair into the eyes of those about Him
with the challenge, "Which of you convinceth Me
of sin?" He who taught His disciples to pray,
"Forgive us our trespasses," never made use of the
supplication in His own behalf. In all the biog-
raphies of the most wonderful character there is

nothing more wonderful than the utter absence of
any sense of wrong-doing. Because He was without sin, the consciousness of guilt can have no place
in the fellowship of His sufferings.

There is another element in human experience
that we may not reckon among "His sufferings."
Though Christ tasted death for every man, He did
not know that which constitutes the bitterness of
death for sinful man. The naturalists have called
attention to the significant fact that animals seem to
have no fear of death. They possess the instinct of
self-preservation, but man adds to that a fear of
dissolution. The reason is that the animals know
nothing of sin. They have no foreboding because
of judgment prophecies in conscience. They have
no memories of lost opportunities and rejected
grace. They have no vain regrets; no anticipations
of consequences. This gives death its somber colors
in the thought of man. But all this was foreign to
the experience of Christ. He was not going out
through the gates of life into an unknown country.
He was not carrying with Him a report of failure
and disobedience. He could say, "It is finished."
He could expect the verdict, "Well done!" He
was returning to the glory which He had with the
Father before the world was. Death, for Him, was

going home. "The sting of death," which is sin, was not an element in "His sufferings."

Having thus cleared our field of vision, we turn to the content of our text. It may seem, after such a process of exclusion, that little is left, but we shall find much land yet to be possessed.

Most frequently the Christian may know "the fellowship of His sufferings" in the hours of temptation. Our common conception of fellowship with Christ is associated with experiences of peace and occasions of blessing. We judge ourselves peculiarly near our Lord in those conditions free from all disturbing influences. The intervals of tranquillity, when "not a wave of trouble rolls across the peaceful breast;" the occasions of joy, when the very laughter of heaven seems to echo in our hearts; the seasons of inspiration, when the soul mounts with wings as do the eagles,—these we have considered the times of fellowship with Christ. But it is good to remember that when we have lost the exaltation of worship; when joy seems only a dim memory of brighter days; when temptations crowd us, making their appeal to what we would be pleased to believe are our necessities,—in such sore straits as these we may know "the fellowship of His sufferings." This assurance has been given:

"For in that he himself hath suffered being tempted, he is able to succor them that are tempted." Our blessed Lord "was in all points tempted like as we are," and, we may well believe that, knowing the sore trials of our weakness, there is never a time when Christ is nearer to His people than in their wilderness experiences.

The great temptation of all history, by common consent called "the temptation," was the fierce struggle of days preceding the inauguration of our Lord's ministry. Not that it was His only trial. No doubt He knew the common allurements of childhood, the universal enticements of youth, and was often sorely tried after His wilderness victory. But there He fought the decisive battle of life, and met the typical temptations of His career. The man who is led of the Spirit and tempted of the devil knows the fellowship of those sufferings. When tempted to prostitute God-given powers to selfish ends, or to place the servants of the flesh upon the throne of the spirit, let us not forget that the same seductive suggestion came to the Captain of our salvation: "Command that these stones become bread." It was enforced by the pressure of hunger and the demand of seeming necessity. Wherever there stands a disciple fronting his appetites, and in his conflict, perhaps, seeming so far from God, let him not forget that he is facing the same foe once conquered by his Lord. Resisting the attempted supremacy of the physical and nourishing the real life on the word that proceedeth out of the mouth of God, we enter the circle of Christ's fellowship.

When tempted to resort to doubtful expedients in the work of life, to secure a hearing and influence by spectacular methods; when our eyes are dazzled by the glare and glitter of the superficial; when the inclination sweeps over us to reach a goal without walking the weary way of work, we are not to imagine that such a condition of mind resisted separates us from our Lord. In such a trial of virtue we have His sympathy. He has not forgotten the time when He debated and rejected the plan of throwing Himself from the pinnacle of the Temple into the midst of the worshipers in the court below. Thus He was tempted to secure acceptance as Messiah. Having suffered being thus tempted, His sympathy encircles the beleaguered disciple.

When strong appeal is made to acquisitiveness, a natural instinct of our humanity; when in a material age wealth is regarded as the badge of success and honored as the instrument of power; when avenues of attainment by questionable means lie

5

stretched out before imagination; when generous and glorious pictures of possible good to be accomplished by our possessions are painted by the tempter; we will not be cast off by the One who, looking out over the kingdom of earth from the mountain height, rejected the promise of them all when offered in exchange for devil worship. The man in business, professional, or official life, who follows the Christ through these common experiences, knows "the fellowship of His sufferings." Nor need we make the mistake of thinking that the higher the life the greater will be the freedom from assault. We may fondly hope for a state of grace even here where temptation shall be unknown. The answer to such a vain imagination is that Christ was tempted. Just in degree as our attainments approximate our ideal, will the character and strength of our temptations rise.

The man who suffers in the cause of right may also enjoy this fellowship. It may seem an anachronism to speak to this comfortable congregaion about anything as antiquated as persecution for righteousness' sake. We thankfully think of that as one of the lost arts. Be not deceived. True there has been a change in form, but with it a survival of the fact. Instead of mutilating the body, society has perfected the finer art of torturing the mind. The thumb-screw has been replaced by the pointed shaft of wit. Instead of confinement of the person, ostracism awaits the offender. The inquisitor's tribunal has been expanded, and now includes the shop and street, the office and parlor. The mediæval inquisitor in monkish mask and gown sleeps in the grave, but the man working with you in the shop or associating with you in business, may suddenly transfix you with a caustic criticism that will hurt for days and perhaps rankle for months. The Pharisees of formality are still with us, ponderously denouncing any manifestation of spontaneity or enthusiasm of religious life that threatens fossilized conditions. The Sadducees of skepticism have their successors, who sound the hewgag of boasted free thought and emancipated life, who brand the restraints of religion as narrowness, and who look with patronizing pity upon the toilers of the kingdom. The high priests of modern society know how to call offenders to account and how to punish those who fail to acknowledge authority. The haughty Roman, who cares for none of these things, still lingers in the world. And with all these the disciple of Christ comes in contact.

Make no mistake. There yet remains an opportunity to attain the last of the beatitudes.

Some one may interject: "You are certainly mistaken. My experience is to the contrary. I have been a Christian for many years, and the fact has never caused me the slightest inconvenience, not to mention suffering. Times have changed." Acknowledge the change, but remember there are two very different reasons why the Christian life is more tolerable in these days. In the first place, the influence of Christ permeates society, and the foes of Christianity are feebler and lacking in the resources of former times. But there is another significant and sorrowful cause for the calm and content of some professed Christians. They are spared by the opposition for the same reason that civilized armies do not harass old men and women and other non-combatants; for the same reason that traitors are not visited with condign punishment after capture by the foe. There are many Christians who are non-combatants; who are lacking in the qualities of aggressive godliness; who by their lives play into the hands of the enemy. Of course such are spared. They are even cherished and exploited. The messages sent to the seven Churches of Asia, recorded in Revelation, reveal the fact that

all of them did not suffer persecution. But the two
conspicuous for fidelity, Smyrna and Philadelphia,
were also pre-eminent in trial. There were two of
those Churches, however, that seemed to be perfectly free from suffering for the sake of their
cause. The lukewarm Church in Laodicea at-
tracted no assault; and the one in Sardis, with a
name to live, but dead, aroused no opposition. Until conditions are ideal the Spirit-filled saint must
be a disturbing influence. The secret of a peaceful
life may be only the shameful impotence of a merely
nominal Christianity.

This review has not exhausted the possibilities
of this fellowship. There was another element in
the sufferings of our Lord which we may share.
He knew what it meant to minister without appreciation and to serve without sympathy. The unappreciated Christ came to His own, and His own received Him not. How different would have been
the story of His life if the chosen people had recognized, welcomed, and supported their Messiah!
What a depth of pathos in His lament: "O Jerusalem, Jerusalem, thou that killest the prophets, and
stonest them which are sent unto thee, how often
would I have gathered thy children together, even
as a hen gathereth her chickens under her wings,

and ye would not!" Even in the Nazareth home there was the same absence of appreciation. Could there have been a deeper humiliation than the effort of His kinsmen to lay hold upon Him, because, as they put it, "He is beside Himself?" They were so lacking in vision that at the time of the episode, they looked upon the glory of history as the shame of the family. The same conditions obtained even in the inner circle of discipleship. It must have been an aggravation even of the agony in the garden, that of the disciples, roused from sleep, He must ask: "Couldest not thou watch one hour?" His life experience would have justified the use of the Psalmist's lament: "Reproach hath broken my heart; and I am full of heaviness; and I looked for some to take pity, and there was none; and that which comforts, but I found none."

Wherever there is a disciple without sympathy in the home; wherever there is a toiler without appreciation from those he seeks to bless; wherever there is a reformer urging an unpopular cause for Christ's sake; there are those who fellowship with the Christ. Of such we know no better type in modern life than those we call foreign missionaries. Describing their hardships, we are apt to speak of absence from home, of rigors of climate, and of perils to life. But one of the heaviest burdens of the lonely workers in the foreign field is lack of human sympathy. They are unappreciated by those they help—objects of suspicion and even hatred. They are unappreciated by those they represent; witness the meager and grudging support given by the Church at home. They are unappreciated by lookers-on; witness the frequent contempt for their work by tourists and government officials. The cup held to the lips of Christ's evangels in foreign fields holds no greater bitterness. For this desire for sympathy is an instinct of human nature. No man is so strong and self-sufficient as not to suffer when it is withheld. Many (of whom the world was not worthy) have had fellowship with the sufferings of the unappreciated Christ.

One more element of this fellowship deserves mention. It is the inevitable sadness that is born of the simple knowledge of human sin and human wretchedness. It is granted that the world's volume of suffering has been greater in times past; that present-day conditions are more distinctly wholesome and conducive to comfort; that more agencies exist for the discovery and relief of acute distress; that the altruistic feeling is far stronger, more generally diffused, and more practical in its aims and

methods.  It is no doubt true that, in proportion to
population, men are better off than in any previous
period of history.  But it is also true that there
has never been a time when the human consciousness of the misery of others was more poignant.
There is more vicarious suffering than ever before;
more sad hearts because of the world's wretchedness; more souls that echo the anguish of the race.
Wherever life has been touched by the Spirit of
Christ this consciousness follows as a result.  The
world knows better to-day than at any point in its
history how to interpret the experience of the Lord
Jesus in the garden of Gethsemane, when He gathered to His heart of love the sin and woe of the
world.

This fellowship with the sufferings of Christ, increasingly characteristic of our era, is due to two
factors.  There is, first, a larger knowledge of conditions.  For the first time in history men constitute, for news purposes, a single community.  Morning and evening, moist and fresh from the press, information of the world's doings and conditions is
spread before us.  We hear the universal cry of sorrow, and it is like the sound of many waters.  Over
mountain and ocean come the appeals of tortured
and outraged Armenians; across the white silences

of far Siberia the imprisoned anguish escapes to
America; from far-off India we hear the weak
moans of the emaciated and dying victims of fam-
ine; up through the social crust sound the groans
and curses of "the submerged tenth;" and from the
Orient we hear the clash of armies, and are touched
by the horrors of war on the other side of the planet.
No human sorrow lies outside the range of knowledge or the circumference of sympathy. In antiq-
uity the Greek or the philanthropic Roman could
not attain the hundredth part of our information
concerning world conditions. The devout of the
Middle Ages, sheltered in cell or cave, might pity
suffering humanity, but how limited his knowledge!
Not until our own generation has the world been
rolled upon the shoulders of a Christian Atlas. Not
until our own time has "earth with its thousand
voices" made its tremendous appeal to the Christian
conscience and the Christian sympathy.

But the simple knowledge would not of itself
produce this world sympathy. If Greek and Roman
had possessed our knowledge they would not have
manifested a race feeling. The pious Jew might
sing his lyric lamentations over the desolations of
his own race, but those outside were dogs. This
new feeling is a fruit of the Spirit of Christ. It is

because men have come into fellowship with the Man of Sorrows that conditions have changed. The kingdom of heaven comes in sympathy and helpfulness. The Christian spirit, imparted to the hearts of men, has brought the Christ-man's burden. This fellowship will grow from more to more. That which we now see is only as the first faint streak of dawn to the full glory of the noon. In spiritual life, as in organic life, it is a law that the lowest forms are least sensitive to suffering; and that the higher you rise in the scale of being the larger the capacity. So more and more, as men become like Him and the world rolls down its way to the feet of the Master, will the cry of human sorrow be heard by "the body of Christ" and answered in sympathy and beneficence. It is not the increase in the amount of human suffering which has depressed some of the finest spirits of the age, and led some of them to believe that the world is growing worse; but it is the growing pressure of the Spirit of Christ making those under its influence more sensitive. And when the glorious day shall dawn, and an expectant world is about to step across the threshold of the millennium, we may believe that the last faint cry of suffering humanity will be answered by a responsive sympathy round the globe.

Let us carry from the sermon one truth, precious to the heart that has recognized some of its own experiences in this study. In the sharing of sufferings there is a mighty and marvelous power that knits heart to heart. Lives seem to flow together and melt into one under the influence of the fiery solvent of adversity. The good fellowship that springs like a mushroom from the soil of common interests and common success, as quickly perishes when conditions change. But the fellowship born of common suffering is as strong as love and as enduring as memory. The surviving soldiers of a gallant regiment, sharing the hardships of the march, the privations of the prison and the horrors of the field, have a fellowship that survives even the firing of the salute at the grave. Those who constitute the sturdy "remnant" of some great reform, standing together against the majority with stone-wall fortitude, or moving together with confident courage in the charge against overwhelming odds, belong to each other by the clear title of fellowship in sufferings. The friends who have walked together in the darkness; who have mingled their tears in common sorrow; who have leaned in times of weakness upon each other's strength; find their hearts cemented together in lasting union. Thus the disciples of Christ, so filled with His Spirit that they think His thoughts, feel something of His emotions, and endeavor to carry on His work in the midst of a suffering world, may reverently think of their relation to Christ and repeat those words of fellowship made sacred by use in the assembly of His people:

"We share our mutual woes,
　　Our mutual burdens bear."

## IV.

## THE MISSION OF THE LITTLE CHILD.

*"And a little child shall lead them."*—Isa. ii, 6.

THE little child holds high rank in the kingdom of heaven. The ancient prophet of Judah, voicing the national hope of the chosen people, found it embodied in a child with a great mission: "Unto us a child is born, unto us a son is given: and the government shall be upon His shoulder: and His name shall be called Wonderful, Counselor, the Mighty God, the Everlasting Father, the Prince of Peace." Centuries afterward the angel of the Lord again announced the coming of a little child with a gracious ministry: "And she shall bring forth a son, and thou shalt call His name Jesus: for He shall save His people from their sins." In anticipation of the birth and the office of the little child, priestly Zacharias sang his *Benedictus;* Mary lifted up her voice in the exultant strains of the *Magnificat;* and the aged and lingering Simeon uttered his *Nunc Dimittis.* Later, above the Judean plains, the advent an-

gels broke the silence of the night with their *Glorias,*
because a little child had been born in the near-by
village, and because its coming was the promise of
peace on earth and good will to men. A typical
scene of the new régime, thus ushered in, is that of
the Christ standing with a little child in His arms,
His hand resting upon the tiny head in blessing. A
typical declaration of the new order is found in the
familiar words: "Suffer the little children to come
unto Me, and forbid them not; for of such is the
kingdom of heaven." A typical command of the
new movement is that given to the great apostle:
"Feed my lambs." The latest period of human history was inaugurated by the coming of a little child
and all events, great and small, of the modern world
are dated from a manger cradle. The most popular anniversary of civilization is that which cele-
brates the birthday of a babe. Verily a new and
beautiful era for childhood dawned at Bethlehem.

This tender regard for little children is a distinguishing feature of the Christian religion. It stands
in striking contrast to the sentiment and practice of
the time in the Roman world. There the inhuman
and revolting custom of exposure, or abandonment,
of poor, female, and defective children had reached
its climax of horror. Latin literature tells us of the

common treatment of the little child. The writers of that decadent time throw many a sidelight upon the sickening conditions. So debased was the moral tone of the existing civilization that parental affection, one of the most powerful of the natural instincts, had been subverted to such a degree that mulitudes of parents abandoned their new-born children, expecting no better fate for them than death by exposure, the evils of slavery, the hell of prostitution, or murder to furnish the materials for the incantations of witches. Against the protests of stoic philosophers and rhetoricians, against the edicts of the more humane of the Roman emperors, and against the outcries of the earliest Christian preachers, the practice persisted. It was conquered only by the forces turned loose in that social order by the Christ, the lover of the little child. The debt of childhood to Christianity seems in no wise exaggerated by the words of the author of "Gesta Christi," when he declared: "Probably of all practical changes which Christianity has encouraged or commenced in the history of the world, this respect and value for children is the most important, as it affects the foundation of all society and government, and influences a far distant future."

But beyond that which Christ wrought for childhood, is the suggestion of our topic, that the little child has a function of its own in the life of the world. We ordinarily regard the child from the viewpoint of parental responsibility. The modern world is asking what it ought to do for the children. This is the question so seriously debated by mothers' clubs and congresses; this is the question of the modern Church which, in the spirit of its Founder, takes the little ones up in its arms; this is the question of modern society, intent upon removing every stumbling-block out of the way of infant feet. Modern literature, like the Magi of old, has placed a rich tribute at the feet of childhood. The poet stoops over the cradle and tries to interpret, with Wordsworth, the passing smiles that lighten the sleeping baby face. Others, touched with the contagion of childlove, have listened to their artless prattle, and have reproduced for us the day-dreams and quaint fancies of the little ones. The words of Amiel, the pensive philosopher, find a ready response in the modern heart: "Blessed be childhood, which brings down something of heaven into the midst of our rough earthliness. These eighteen thousand daily births of which statistics tell us, represent as it were an effusion of innocence and freshness, struggling not only against the death of the race, but against human corruption and the universal gangrene of sin." And ever the perennial baby-lover, the young mother, passing rich with her new-found treasure, studies the budding life clasped in her arms and ponders her sweet and strange discoveries in her heart. But while our library shelves groan under the weight of volumes recording the great deeds of great men; books telling of what men and women have done to ease the burdens on weary shoulders and to illuminate the pathways of progress for stumbling feet; books warning the adult world of its duty to childhood and suggesting the ways and means of its discharge; no one seems to have taken in hand the genial task of setting forth the mission of the little child. The attempt reveals unexpected riches in material.

"And a little child shall lead them." The comment offered by the latest science upon the ancient prophecy is more like a fairy tale than the usual dry and measured findings of a scientific report. As the wise men of the East, representatives of the science of their time, under the guidance of the star sought the place where an infant lay, so their successors, the scientists of the West, seeking knowledge, though of a different sort and from a different motive, have again been guided to the cradle of the lit-

6

tle child. The grave investigator has fallen under
"the spell of the baby," and is sitting reverently at
its feet in his search for truth. Using the historical
method he goes back as far as possible towards the
genesis of things. The same kind of curiosity that
turns from the mastodon and places the infusoria
under the microscope; that deserts the towering
form of the California redwood to study the lichen
on the rock; that prompts the geologist to reproduce
in theory the first stages in the building up of our
planet; that studies the embryo rather than the developed organism; has impelled the student of man
to the study of the child. So rich and varied is
the significance of the little child to science that
we are told that it is "a monument of the race" and
"a key to its history." It is difficult, we are told, to
exaggerate the importance of the little child to the
modern savant, for the reason that he finds preserved in its experiences and changes the history of
primitive man. Even the psychologists have set a
little child in the midst, fastening attention upon
consciousness in the germ, and seeking a richer
knowledge of the mind of man by means of the mental activities of the infant. Here, too, they tell us,
is reproduced in miniature a résumé of the slow upward progress of the species, and the unwritten his-

tory of the race-mind is found in the development
of the child-mind. Thus the little child is leading
the seekers for knowledge, and the old prophecy
finds an unexpected fulfillment.

Special interest attaches to the fact that the most
important contribution made to science by the late
Professor John Fiske was his exposition of the mission of the little child. In his little volume, "The
Destiny of Man," he points out that the prolonged
period of infancy has released man from the bondage of heredity, a bondage so complete in the animal world that it forbids all progress, making each
generation a replica of that which it succeeds. He
declares that it was the little child that led the parents away from self, and guided them out into fields
of thought and action that were not purely self-re-
garding. He further asserts that with the little
child there came to the race teachableness, individ-
uality, and a capacity for progress, which are the
peculiar prerogatives of the fully developed man.
Speaking the sober and carefully weighed words of
science, he affirms that human childhood contains
"the germ of all that is pre-eminent in humanity,"
and that it is the guaranty of man's boundless pro-
gressiveness. How great has been the mission of
the little child, according to this master of scientific

exposition, let us state in his own words from his "Cosmic Philosophy:" "From of old ye have heard the monition, 'Except ye be as babes ye can not enter the kingdom of heaven;' the latest science now shows us—though in a very different sense of the words—that unless we had been as babes, the ethical phenomena which gives all its significance to the phrase 'kingdom of heaven,' would have been non-existent for us. Without the circumstances of infancy, we might have become more formidable among animals through sheer force of sharp-wittedness. But except for these circumstances we should never have comprehended the meaning of such phrases as 'self-sacrifice' and 'devotion.' The phenomena of social life would have been omitted from the history of the world, and with them the phenomena of ethics and religion." After such a statement as this by an accredited spokesman, let no one imagine the ancient prophet guilty of an extravagance born of religious ecstasy when he says: "And a little child shall lead them."

The same high appreciation of the mission of the little child characterizes the notable Lowell lectures by the late Professor Henry Drummond, published under the title of "The Ascent of Man." The poetry, the science, and the religion of the subject are beautifully commingled. In a chapter, bearing the startling caption, "The Evolution of a Mother" —a chapter that is unique in literature—he describes in detail the mission of a little child. Reversing the common conception of the child as the offspring of the mother, he describes the function of the little child as the prime factor in producing the mother. This is declared to be the most stupendous task ever committed to the hands of evolution. The mother is nature's supreme achievement. All the processes of organic nature looked forward to this one great end, and at the top of the scale of animal life you find the mothers. "Ask the zoologist," says the author, "what, judging from science alone, Nature aspired to from the first, he could but answer Mammalia—mothers."

But by what means was this consummation achieved? To what factor, from the scientist's point of view, is the world indebted for the mother? Without hesitation the answer is given: "To create motherhood and all that enshrines itself in that holy word, required a human child." This human necessity finds its explanation in the fact that among the lower animals the children are not really children at all; they are merely and literally offspring— springers-off; their advent is followed by imme-

diate desertion; in quick forgetfulness of their ma-
ternity they set up in the business of life for themselves. The influences that radiate from the child
after birth, which are the creative human influences,
are wholly lacking. To give these opportunity is
needed the prolonged period of infancy. In Professor Drummond's own words: "No greater day
ever dawned for evolution than this on which the
first human child was born. For then entered into
the world the one thing wanting to complete the
ascent of man—a tutor for the affections." Beyond
this even reaches the mission of the little child. Cit-
ing the fact that "it is the mature opinion of every
one who has thought upon the history of the world,
that the thing of highest importance for all times
and to all nations is family life," the author makes
two statements, startlingly significant. The first is
that baby fingers bound together the two essential
elements in the creation of home; that the father
and mother have been united and are held in holy,
lasting, heart-to-heart union only in the love of a
little child. The second statement, a confirmation of
the first, based on the history of the family, is to the
effect that love for children is always a prior and a
stronger thing than love between parents. In brief,
it is the dictum of modern science that the physical,

social, civil, and moral redemption of the human race waited for the coming of a little child. In the beginning of human history, multiplied millenniums away from its goal, it was evidently written: "And a little child shall lead them."

The mission of the little child is not exhausted in the broad outlines already given. Beyond its function as a factor in social evolution; beyond the doctrine of the Incarnation, whose content is the mission of the little child in redemption; beyond these things is the ministry of childhood in the personal life. Here it is first of all our privilege to think of the little child as a gift of God, a messenger of heavenly love, a token of divine favor. We cherish the thought that in the fullness of time God sent the human child to start the race upon its journey of progress, for "evolution is God's way of doing things," and He furnishes forces and factors. We believe that God sent the Bethlehem babe, "for God so loved the world, that He gave His only begotten Son, that whosoever believeth in Him might not perish, but have everlasting life." Then God save us from the pitiful skepticism which doubts that the fresh stream of infancy continually flowing into an ever-aging world, comes from the hand of Him who is the Giver of every good gift! These little ones of our own hearts and homes come to us on a mission divine. Poetry has clothed this beautiful truth in words that are as "apples of gold in pictures of silver." Thus Wordsworth, in his ode on "Immortality," describes the nativity of our babes:

> "Not in entire forgetfulness,
> And not in utter nakedness,
> But trailing clouds of glory do we come
> From God, who is our home;
> Heaven lies about us in our infancy."

Faith, as expressed in the old Hebrew hymn, sees in the little child a messenger of divine love: "Lo, children are a heritage of the Lord: and the fruit of the womb is His reward." Revelation, as it fell from the lips of the Christ, makes the same gladly solemn announcement: "And He took a child and set him in the midst of them; and when He had taken him in His arms, he said unto them, Whosoever shall receive one of such children in My name, receiveth Me; and whosoever shall receive Me, receiveth not Me, but Him that sent Me." Let us believe that it was a true instinct that led the childless Hebrew wife of old to feel that she had been denied the coronal glory of womanhood; that influenced her to lay her sorrow on the altar of God's house, and to pray for a little child as a mark of divine favor; that caused her to welcome her babe as a gift from above and to give it the name Samuel—"heard of the Lord;" that brought her back to the holy place to lay her sacrifice of thanksgiving on the altar jeweled with her tears.

The speechless babe brings its own message of love from the Father in heaven to the mother and father of earth. The child, in itself, is a token of the divine desire to bless the home into which it comes. The child, in itself, is the divinely appointed means by which the wife shall taste the highest joy that comes to womanhood. The child, in itself, is the factor by which the lives of mother and father are enriched and made complete. The child, in itself, is the assurance that Christ comes knocking at the door of the home. And if we have fallen upon a time when the little child is not welcome in our lives; if it is becoming increasingly true that its high mission is not appreciated; if in the present social conditions increasing luxury, engrossing business, love of pleasure, and desire for ease shut the door of the so-called home in the face of the little ones, we have fallen upon a time when men and women are wronging their own souls, and are missing the beatitude of the parent.

This truth is emphasized when we consider the

ministry of childhood in another aspect. The interpretations of the passage, of which our text is a
fragment, swing between far extremes. Some, like
Dr. George Adam Smith, insist that the statements
must be understood literally; that when Isaiah
speaks of beasts he means beasts; that the conflict
between man and the animal, like the alienation of
man from God and the antagonisms of man and his
fellows, will disappear under the benign influences
of the Messianic reign. The key to the words of
Paul, "The earnest expectation of the creature wait-
eth for the manifestation of the sons of God," is
found in the prophecy that right relations between
man and beast will be restored only by the processes
of redemption. On the contrary, there are those
who present an allegorical interpretation. When
we read that "the wolf shall dwell with the lamb,
and the leopard shall lie down with the kid, and the
calf with the lion, and a little child shall lead them,"
they refuse to accept a zoological meaning. They
argue that it is not the purpose of the prophet to
describe the effects of redemption on animal life.
But we are to see in the wolf, the leopard, and the
lion representatives of the cruel and violent appetites and passions of human nature. These wild
beasts are appropriate figures in which an imagina-

tion, not Oriental in its type, might set forth the
malevolent forces at work in society. This passage,
according to this view, is a Gospel promise that
these preying and destroying tempers will be sub-
dued under the reign of the Prince of Peace.

Without pausing to choose between these interpretations, either of which adds new desire to our
prayer, "Thy kingdom come," we simply mark the
fact, witnessed by experience and observation, that
the little child does exercise what may be reverently
and without exaggeration called a regenerating influence. Regeneration means to us being "born
again" into a higher life. Thus we are "born again"
into the kingdom of God. But there are other trans-
formations in experience analogous to the great
change by which a man becomes a new creature in
Christ Jesus. Human nature is charged with latent capacities and possibilities. They are not developed at birth, but must be awakened to life and
incited to action by outside influences. This is true
of many of our affections. The true husband lives
a higher life than the solitary man, and the true
wife knows a higher life than the single woman.
But we are not born husbands and wives; in attain-
ing this higher life we are "born again." Man becomes a true husband and woman becomes a true

wife when the conjugal affections, hitherto dormant, are quickened into life by the touch of another human spirit. Above the man is the husband, and above the husband is the father. Above the woman is the wife, and above the wife is the mother. But the parent is not born. Like the Christian he must be born again. We do not come into life equipped with parental affection except in capacity. The physical and spiritual possibilities of fatherhood and motherhood may be present, but in the absence of the little child we can never enter the kingdom of parental love. We are led through the gates of this earthly paradise by infant hands. Baby fingers place the crown of motherhood upon every woman's brow.

Who will deny this transforming influence of the little child? Under the touch of infant life the merry girl is transformed into a Madonna—a holy mother; charming with the beauty of girlhood, she becomes radiant with the glory of motherhood. Her chastened face glows with the light of a great love, the purest and strongest next to the love of God. Then come thoughtfulness, and sympathy, and patience, and sacrifice, with a beauty of their own, more compelling and enduring than the mere physical charm of budding womanhood. Since day unto day uttereth such speech of the perpetual ministry of the little child, we read with fresh appreciation the words of Professor Drummond: "When the first mother awoke to her first tenderness and warmed her loneliness at her infant's love, when for a moment she forgot herself and thought upon its weakness or its pain, when by the most imperceptible act or sign or look of sympathy she expressed the unutterable impulse of motherhood, the touch of a new creative hand was felt upon the world." It is the little child, too, that transforms the mere man into the higher product of a father. The evolutionist tells us that when nature undertook to make fathers out of lawless savages the task was committed to infant hands. That service, accomplished for the race, is repeated in greater or less degree for the individual man. The love for his new-born child counteracts the nomadic instincts of man's primitive ancestors and holds him within the softening atmosphere of home. The same regenerating influence quickens his protective and fostering instincts, wakens mighty affections in his heart, reveals to his wondering gaze unsuspected depths of tenderness in his nature, gives a permanent impulse to industry, and produces qualities of character in masculine nature that add beauty to strength as the art of olden times placed lily work upon the tops of the pillars.

The mission of the little child, in thus giving us mothers and fathers and laying the foundations of home, reaches from this domestic center to a social circumference that would carry us too far a-field in its exploration. We may only mention the suggestive fact that Mr. Spencer and others have indicated, how the direct influence of the little child, exerted in the limited sphere of the household, has reacted upon the social affections of the race and has been a factor in developing our pitifulness for all weak and helpless things. The child is not a pauper burdening the charity of the world; it is an angel of the grace of God bestowing exceeding abundantly beyond value received.

Reluctantly putting to one side other tempting phases of this fascinating subject we give consideration to just one more. Thus far we have traced a sweeping movement, extending all the long way from the nethermost depths of savagery to the uppermost heights of parental affection, where the mountain peaks of our humanity seem to catch the glow of light from another world. In the pages of the book of life already turned we have found, to quote the happy phrase of Drummond, "a love story." What is the nature of the closing chapter? Does it end as all love stories ought to end? Our first thought answers with a negative. The little child, nestling in our arms or climbing upon our knees, is not a permanent possession. We lose our children in two ways. They grow to manhood or womanhood, or, lingering long enough to grip our hearts with their dimpled fingers, they die. Over every bright and beautiful scene upon which our eyes have rested in this panoramic survey the shadow of death falls soon or late. One of the mysteries of nature is the profusion of blossoms that never fulfill the promise of fruit. One of the bitterest mysteries of human experience is Rachel weeping for her children. When the little child passes on into the invisible does that mean only the frustration of awakened hopes, the beneficent purpose unfulfilled, the end of its mission? The human judgment is witnessed by the marble column broken in twain, a symbol by which we declare that the life was unfinished; that the career was only a fragment. But the popular verdict, based simply on duration in time is worthless. Threescore years and ten do not complete a life. Though we labor until we bend under the weight of years; though we climb to the last round of ambition's ladder; though we drink to the last drop of the cup of joy; we leave behind us unfinished work and carry with us unrealized ideals. History gives record of but one career that could be signalized at its close by the words, "It is finished," and that was the life of a young man.

We are prone to omit a factor from the problem. There is another life. Beyond time stretches eternity; over the earth rises heaven; beyond life lies immortality. We are pilgrims marching through mortality toward immortality following the star of hope. Here we have no continuing city, but we seek one to come. The event of the little child's transplanting must be viewed in its relation to two worlds. Just as God sent his angel of life, in the guise of the babe, to create the family and to found the home on earth fair and full of promise, may we not believe that the child has a mission in leading our reluctant feet toward the eternal home in heaven, and fitting us for the higher life that dwells therein? Are we not entitled to the comfort of the poet's calm trust:

> " That Life is ever lord of Death,
> And Love can never lose its own!"

For we can not rest in the thought of broken lines of progress. All these great world-processes, leading ever to higher and yet higher life, come to a pitiful anti-climax if they terminate at the tomb. It is the reassuring message of our time, as it has been the burden of the Gospel from the beginning, that death serves the end of life. And when we remember that our Lord, comforting His disciples in prospect of their coming bereavement, said, "It is expedient for you that I go away," may not that same loving purpose be fulfilled in other losses? If the Christ could do more for His loved ones by departing than by longer walking at their side, may it not be true that the little child's ministry of blessing is continued after it passes through the gates?

This has been the blessed lesson many have been taught in tears and loneliness. The little child comes to the home, and love stands at the door with its welcome. It touches hearts with a heavenly magic. Hosts of pure and mighty affections spring into being. Love guards the cradle and happiness sits at the fireside. But another day and the little minister returns to "the service of the inner shrine." But, thank God, the babes can not go back to heaven and leave us as though they had never come into our lives. The new-born affections do not die. There are no cemeteries where sorrowing mothers and fathers bury love under withering flowers,

7

Then comes a new ministry. The darling in the home adds to our peace and contentment here; but the little one in heaven becomes a magnet drawing its lovers upward. Those who have thought of heaven as a foreign country now sit to hear what the faithful Witness reveals of its glories. The Christ has a claim upon our devotion as we think of Him as taking our own into His tender care. We grope in the darkness of sorrow along the way the little feet have passed. Of many pilgrims with their faces toward the city of God it might be written: "A little child shall lead them." May the Father give all bereaved parents the poet's vision:

> "Here at the portal thou dost stand,
>     And with thy little hand
> Thou openest the mysterious gate
>     Into the future's undiscovered land."

# V.

## THE REMEMBRANCER.

*"But the Comforter, even the Holy Spirit, whom
the Father will send in My name, He shall teach
you all things, and bring to your remembrance
all that I said unto you."*—John xiv, 26. (R. V.)

A RECENT writer on psychological subjects proposes a new definition of memory. It is that department of mental life about which everybody has
been talking for hundreds of years, without telling
us anything which persons of common sense did
not already know. The fact of memory lies on the
surface. From the time of the Greek philosophers
to the publication of the latest hand-book on psychology, men have described its phenomena and catalogued its conditions. But, while many ingenious
theories have been offered in explanation of its
workings, its problems remain unsolved. The best
account to be given of memory, to date, is that God
has so constituted us that our minds have this peculiar power. The best descriptions still distinguish

its threefold activity of retention, reproduction, and recognition. The first of these terms represents a sort of photographic quality of mind by which it retains pictures of past experiences; reproduction indicates the ability of the mind to make copies from a negative once taken; while recognition stands for the fact that we are able to refer the copies to their originals—to recognize them as reproductions of that which we have once seen, or heard, or felt, or thought.

But, baffled by the mysteries of memory, we must acknowledge the fundamental importance of its practical functions. It is essential to all intelligent mental activity. Without memory we could maintain no sovereignty over the province of the past. The passing moment, or, to speak more accurately, about ten seconds, would be the measure of known existence; each separate instant would be a lifetime, with no connection with aught before or after; wisdom, the product of the passing years, could never reach its harvest time; and history would perpetually perish at the moment of its birth. Without memory there could be no such thing as individual experience. The materials out of which it is built would be taken from us at the instant of production; events would leave no more impression upon us than is made by the passing moon upon the placid waters of the lake; and, hence, there could be no organization of the products of past feeling, thought, and sense into anything entitled to be known as experience. Without memory there could be no development of the individual. The child would never be able to conquer the alphabet; the artisan would have to begin each moment to learn his trade anew; and the scholar could never put more than one foot across the threshold of the temple of knowledge. Without memory all human relations would be disrupted. The mother would immediately lose sight of her babe; the husband parting from his wife would meet her again as an utter stranger; friendship would be eternally banished from the land of forgetfulness; and "the communion of the saints" would be nothing but a meaningless phrase. Without memory there could be no moral character. Duty would cease to exist where the knowledge of obligation, like Noah's dove, could find no resting place in the life; the occupation of conscience, with its approval of the right and its condemnation of the wrong, would be gone if the mind kept no record of the deeds done in the body; while attainment would forever fly before us like a startled wild bird at the sound of approaching footsteps. Without memory man would be literally a lost soul. There would be no basis left even for personal identity, for memory alone can certify to us the fact that we have existed at any previous moment.

Few studies are more interesting than those which have to do with the religious functions of natural faculties. Such investigations are also practical. They bring religion down from the upper air and domesticate it in the very heart of life. In one vital aspect salvation is a human achievement. Working out our own salvation brings every faculty of our nature into action. Seeing how life, in all its rich and high significance, hangs upon the beneficent ministry of memory, we realize that this marvelous faculty holds an important office in the economy of redemption. The description of the functions of memory already given indicates its religious uses. The Christian is vitally related to the past, to experience, to development, to social intercourse, and to moral character, and these relations depend on memory. We are, therefore, gratified to find among the treasures of our religion an aid to memory. This is offered in the prophetical promise of our text: "But the Comforter, even the Holy Spirit, whom the Father will send in My name, he shall . . . bring to your remembrance all that I said unto you." Like all promises and prophecies, this one must be studied in the light of history and experience. Thus we trace the fulfillment of the prophecy and confirm our faith in the promise.

This pledge of necessity, had a peculiar and unique relation to the little circle of hearers who heard it for the first time. We have a reasonable expectation of finding the first fulfillment of its prophecy in their experience. Looking backward we can see the imperative necessity of such a provision in their case. Those men were to be forever the teachers of the whole world in things pertaining to Christ. They were to preach His Gospel. They were to produce His literature. They were to meet His antagonists. Their minds were to be the depositories of the historic and didactic materials of Christianity. As witnesses to Christ a primary necessity would be fidelity of recollection. In view of their high mission no imaginable aid could be of greater value than the gift of special remembrance. Without such assistance they would surely fail to make a faithful report of the Lord's teachings, or to give to the world an adequate narrative of His life. As Dean Alford has said: "It is on the fulfillment of this promise to the apostles that their sufficiency as witnesses of all the Lord did and taught, and consequently the authenticity of the Gospel narrative, is grounded." By virtue of this promise we read the Gospel teachings with confidence, and we receive as authoritative their expansion and explanation in the epistles. We have here a voucher for something higher than human memory and human reflection in their contents.

The value of the promise can be appreciated only in the light of existing conditions. A fundamental necessity for this reminding office of the Spirit is seen to exist in the disciples themselves. They had been receiving a preparatory education for their stupendous task. Their training began after they had reached adult years. Their receptive powers had been weakened by acquired habits of thought, by the prejudices of a different education, and by the traditions of a splendid history. In the presence of Christ they found themselves in a new and strange atmosphere. They move through the Gospel pages in a sort of spiritual stupor. It is a commonplace that they did not understand the words of Christ. They grossly misconceived His divine mission. Their ideals were of the earth, earthy. The part they play in the four Gospels does not arouse the slightest admiration for their intellectual abili-

ties or spiritual qualities. They were certainly unpromising material out of which to produce world
leadership. The superficial reader can understand
that some great transformation must have taken
place in the disciples before they became fit vessels
to carry the heavenly treasure to all mankind.

But such were the students in that traveling
theological school as they finished their three years'
course. Does any one ask why the Master did not
have them thoroughly equipped for their work when
He delivered His valedictory address in the upper
room? The answer is simplicity itself. The acqui-
sition of knowledge depends upon two factors—
the ability of the teacher and the capacity of the
pupil. The primary question in education is not,
How much does the teacher know? but, How much
can the scholar grasp? The simple communication
of so much truth does not make the recipient immediately and proportionately knowing. Knowledge
is a growth, and not a hypodermic injection. The
teacher must always adjust himself to the attainments and the ability of the disciple. The great
Teacher observed the fundamental laws of development and progress in the training of those who
were to be His successors in bringing men to the
knowledge of God.

This accommodation to the limited capacity of the disciples is sometimes stated in the narrative in so many words. In this last discourse the Master said to them: "I have many things to say unto you, but ye can not bear them now." The metaphor is that of a crushing weight which might be placed upon physical weakness. The limitation was not in the knowledge of the Teacher, but in the capacity of the taught. The reticence was born of a loving consideration for human frailty. There were some revelations they could not have borne in the earlier stages of their instruction. Suppose that in their weakness they had understood that the new movement would result in the eclipse of the Mosaic dispensation, the discontinuance of the ancient forms of worship, and the death of the national hope of visible empire? Devoted Jews could only stand such a revelation when girded with the new spiritual power of Christianity, and when their old patriotism had risen to the higher devotion of the kingdom of God. Suppose that, in their bigotry and prejudice, they had realized the catholic nature of the new order; that the kingdom of Christ would admit Gentiles to its privileges on equal terms; that the blood of Abraham would give no advantage to those who made it their pride and boast? That truth had to be communicated to Peter in a heavenly vision. Only when thoroughly committed to Christ and filled with His Spirit, were they ready to throw wide open the gates of salvation and cry, "Whosoever will." Even when the note of universality was sounded by way of remembrance, a struggle ensued before Christianity gained recognition among the disciples as anything larger than a Jewish sect. The new lesson, like the ancient law, was weak through the flesh.

The method of the instruction, governed by the conditions just described, also emphasizes the importance of the office of remembrance committed to the Spirit. The teaching of our Lord was not methodical. Only a limited part of it was in set discourses. Its treasures are found in personal interviews, transient conversations, puzzling paradoxes, occasional repartee, responses to appeals, corrections of errors, answers to questions, denunciations of wickedness, consolations of affliction, and sympathy with sorrow. One of the Master's favorite forms of instruction is the parable. This both reveals and conceals the truth. An exposition of a parable was rarely given. They waited to unfold their stores of information by the way of remembrance. In keeping with this purpose are words spoken upon this occasion: "These things have I spoken to you in proverbs; but the time cometh when I shall no more speak unto you in proverbs, but show you plainly of the Father." The truths only partially intelligible, or wholly forgotten, would in memory reveal the hidden meaning with which they were laden. Out of this apparent confusion of utterance the Divine Remembrancer at a fitting time would bring to memory all that had been spoken by the Master.

One more reason why the efficacy of Christ's teachings waited upon remembrance is found in its large element of prediction. That which was anticipatory must of necessity defer interpretation until the event. The doctrines of Christianity are founded upon historical facts. The history deposited the materials of the doctrines, and the understanding of much of the teaching depended upon the completion of a course of events still in progress. The facts had to be in hand before they could be expounded or applied. How true this is can be seen in a Scriptural statement of a fundamental doctrine: "Christ died for our sins." "Christ died"— that is the historical fact; "Christ died for our sins" —that is the Christian doctrine. The doctrine would be worthless without the fact; and the doctrine must wait for the fact. This feature of His teaching, as

dependent upon the future, was recognized by
Christ. Again and again He said: "I have told
you before it come to pass, that when it comes to
pass ye may believe." Such cryptic utterances as
those about the Son of man being lifted up as was
the serpent in the wilderness, the destruction of the
Temple and the raising of it again in three days,
the shedding of His blood for many for the remission of sins, the giving of living water that should
spring up into eternal life, all needed the future
event for their elucidation. The perplexity of the
disciples at the time of the utterance of such statements was natural under the circumstances. But
we have their own explanation of how the splendor
of truth came to their minds later: "When He was
risen from the dead, His disciples remembered that
He spake this, and they believed the Scripture and
the word which Jesus said." And in another connection they tell us how they came to a knowledge
of the truth by way of remembrance: "These things
understood not His disciples at the first, but when
Jesus was glorified then remembered they that these
things were written of Him, and that they had done
these things unto Him."

The Acts of the Apostles is a noble commentary
upon our text. Under the influence of the Spirit

that which had been adjourned to a future time of remembrance now became living knowledge in the minds of the disciples. By virtue of the reminding office of the Comforter there came a rich fulfillment of the Master's prediction: "What I do thou knowest not now, but thou shalt know hereafter." Under the inspiration of the Remembrancer the meanings of Christ's teachings emerged from the mists; the spiritual stupidity of the disciples vanished; the perplexities of their schooldays flashed into light; and the dull, slow students were transformed into energetic, enthusiastic teachers, whose words have engaged the reverent attention of the world's best intellect for nineteen centuries. By the power of the Spirit the stupid, sluggish followers became fearless, forceful leaders, and gave succeeding generations a magnificent object lesson of Christianity in action. Because of this divine gift of remembrance by the Spirit the multitudes heard a noble preaching of the Gospel, and the world holds in its hands the unique literature which embodies the mind of Christ and makes men wise unto salvation. All the achievements of the apostolic age are in evidence as to the accomplishment of the prophecy of the text.

This promise is not to be regarded as the monopoly of the little circle to which it was immediately spoken. The Church universal has appropriated as its own the wealth of our Lord's last discourse. "Let not your heart be troubled" belongs to us all; "I go to prepare a place for you" is a personal message to each member of the household of faith; "I will not leave you comfortless" is the consolation of all the sons of God; "My peace I give unto you" is the legacy of all those who trust in Christ. Our rights in these exceeding great and precious promises are uncontested. But in the midst of this farewell address is the affirmation of our text: "He shall bring to your remembrance all that I said unto you." Consistency will not permit us to designate this as a special favor granted to the first disciples, and at the same time appropriate all the other gracious offerings of the same discourse. The promise contains no time limit. It carries the assurance of a perpetual unfolding of the germinal principles of Christ's teaching, both for the Church and for the individual. It guarantees a spiritual guidance superior to that of an official hierarchy, ecclesiastical tradition, or general revelation. The living Spirit, whose mission it is to glorify Christ, is our Remembrancer.

The history of the Christian Church pays its

tribute to the truth of the text. Its pages disclose a persistent tendency on the part of the Church to forget essential truths taught by Christ. The psychologists tell us that those things are best remembered which are most recent, most interesting, best attended to, and most often repeated. With the passage of time the teachings of Christ would naturally fade from memory. With the loss of interest, consequent upon failure to maintain the vitalities of Christian experience, the hold upon fundamental doctrines gradually weakens. With lack of attention, caused by indifference to duty or by want of opportunity to hear, forgetfulness of the truth follows as the night the day. With the absence of repetition, when preachers cease to expound the Gospel fundamentals, they disappear first from the experience, and then from the beliefs of the people. All this has actually come to pass in the history of the Christian centuries. With the lapse of time, the decay of spiritual life, and the perversions of the Church, some of the teachings of Christ have been lost to remembrance. The perils of faith have always been from neglect within and never from assault without.

But such losses have not been permanent. The records show a perpetual process of recovery. The teachings of Christ have been safeguarded by an agency superior to the unaided human memory. The resurrection of buried truth is one of the recurrent miracles of the years of our Lord. The history of Christian doctrine has numerous chapters which are luminous commentaries upon our theme.

Some of the great landmarks of Church history bear the inscription of the text in letters of light. Witness the Reformation in Europe. The doctrine of justification by faith, as expounded by the Apostle Paul, is found in germ in the teachings of Christ. It is among the things which "began to be spoken by the Lord." It shines like a jewel in the setting of the familiar verse: "For God so loved the world that He gave His only begotten Son, that whosoever believeth in Him should not perish, but have everlasting life." It is the very essence of the parable of the Prodigal Son. This doctrine was emphasized and enforced in the apostolic writings in such manner that no one would have dreamed, before the fact, that it could be lost. But the fifteenth century found the Church operating under a system from which this fundamental truth was missing. Works had usurped the function of faith; penance was playing the part of repentance; human merit was counterfeiting divine grace, and indulgences

8

were on the market as a substitute for the forgiveness of sins. A great Christian doctrine had been forgotten.

But the prophecy of divine remembrance was fulfilled. Dr. Martin Luther embodied the genius of the mighty religious movement first in his own experience. He was reminded that the true ground of justification is not works, but faith; he was reminded that access to God is not by penance, but by repentance; he was reminded that salvation is not secured by human merit, but that it is bestowed by divine grace. Through Him the Spirit spoke to a forgetful world, and brought to the remembrance of men the lost doctrine of divine grace. The sixteenth century found the world ringing with the good news and Germany aflame with zeal in behalf of the recovered teaching of Christ. The Reformation was not the product of new truth. It was the natural outgrowth of the revival in memory and experience of the teaching of Christ and the doctrine of the apostles.

Kindred in its genesis was the evangelical revival in England in the eighteenth century. The influence of the Reformation was a spent force. The kingdom presented a scene of moral degradation and spiritual desolation. It has been described as "an age of religion without faith, of politics without honor, and of life without morality." The indescribable depths into which England had fallen are mirrored in the literature of the period, but can best be seen in Hogarth's pictures and in John Wesley's journals. The Church was stagnant and society was corrupt. The fox-hunting parson had forgotten his message, and the joy of salvation had disappeared from the lives of the people. In the England of Wesley's day a Christian doctrine had been forgotten. Again the Spirit did His work of remembrance. Luther witnessed to justification by faith, but Wesley's message given by the Spirit went a step beyond that: "Therefore being justified by faith, we have peace with God through our Lord Jesus Christ, by whom also we have access by faith into this grace wherein we stand, and rejoice in hope of the glory of God." With his own heart "strangely warmed," he was commissioned of the Spirit to bring back to the memories of men the lost truth of a conscious salvation. It was not a new doctrine but the blessed apostolic truth dropped from remembrance in a period of spiritual decadence.

A striking confirmation of the Spirit's fidelity as a Remembrancer is seen in the history of the Great

Commission.  So prone is memory to let slip essential things that the Church of the living God actually forgot its business.  The last command of our Lord, peculiarly binding and sacred, faded from remembrance and dropped out of the program of Christian activity.  The duty of going and teaching all nations, enjoined under the most solemn and impressive circumstances, perished from the mind of the Church.  The magnificent conception of world conquest, embodying the very genius of our religion, was lost to view.  So thoroughly had the missionary idea departed from Christian thinking, that, when the Spirit of remembrance found a voice in the hero of Paulersburg, a Sydney Smith, a man who had received "holy orders," could characterize the revival of our Lord's farewell commission as "the dream of a dreamer who dreams that he has been dreaming."  Since that time the Church has been stirred up by way of remembrance.  As a result of the resurrection of the lost teaching of Christ the work of the foreign missionary furnished the great apologetic of the nineteenth century; the world has witnessed the influence of Christianity in contact with heathenism as it has not been seen since the first centuries; and the world-wide activities bear witness that the promise of the Lord Jesus has again been fulfilled. But even now we make a distinction between the Christian spirit and the missionary spirit, and we still operate missionary societies within the Churches and cordially and unsuccessfully invite professing Christians to unite and co-operate in obeying our Lord's last command.

Noting with profound gratitude the mission of the Spirit to memory in these great world movements, we must not lose sight of the way of remembrance in individual Christian life. It is a significant thing that life's highest lessons are rarely learned at the time of event. The experience may be most valuable, but its instruction is ministered by memory after the event is past. There are many things that, like the first disciples, we can only know in remembrance. The reasons for this postponement of understanding are readily grasped. Some of our most wholesome lessons are taught in the school of affliction. But when passing through such experiences the mind is agitated and the emotions overwhelm judgment. Deliberate reflection, impartial judgment, clearness of vision, appreciation of advantage, are all impossible when the eyes are dim and the heart is heavy. The interpretation of God's ways must be adjourned until the time when all the materials are at hand, and the person interested is

in a state of mind qualifying him to deal fairly with
them.   At the time we see through a glass darkly;
at first we know only in part, and that part is the
dark, forbidding aspect.   Later we may be able to
say with God's ancient servant: "It is good for me
that I have been afflicted."   The Remembrancer may
bring to memory the loving message of the event,
and help us to recognize the unseen hand of blessing.

Analogous to the recovery of lost doctrines by
the Church is the familiar experience of the remembrance of forgotten truth by the individual in some
hour of need.   At the time Christ spoke in the counsels of a father, the instruction of a Sunday-school
teacher, the example of a friend, or the ministry of
the pulpit, the message was quickly forgotten.   But
who has not known in his own life the resurrection
power of the Spirit in raising buried truth from the
tomb of forgetfulness?   Words, quickly lost, are
suddenly remembered and come back with the force
of conviction.   Bible verses, "committed to memory" as a child, return with startling vividness and
power.   We have found such remembrances
strangely appropriate to our circumstances.   Familiar passages of Scripture so thoroughly our property that we can not recall the time we first received
them, under changed conditions are seen in a new

light, disclose a larger meaning, and seem like a
fresh inspiration from heaven. And who shall say
that they are not as long as we have the promise:
"He shall bring to your remembrance all that I said
unto you?"

Time remains for but one more of the many sug-
gestions of this rich text. As far as we can judge,
the prophecy of this passage will never be finally
fulfilled. Many of the ministries of the Holy Spirit
will cease. The time will come when He shall no
more "reprove the world of sin, and of righteousness, and of judgment," because the day will dawn
when every knee shall bow and every tongue confess
that Jesus Christ is Lord to the glory of God the
Father. The time will come when His tender offices
of comfort will be completed; for God shall gather
all His people into the new city, and "shall wipe
away all tears from their eyes; and there shall be
no more death, neither sorrow, nor crying, neither
shall there be any more pain." The time will come
when His function as a teacher shall finally serve its
divine purpose, and His pupils shall see no longer
"through a glass darkly," but "face to face;" when
they shall know no longer in part, but even as also
they are known. The time will come when His
sanctifying influences will fully accomplish their

work; for there hastens an hour when the sons of God shall be like him, their Example, and when the body of Christ shall be "a glorious Church, not having spot, or wrinkle, or any such thing," and shall be presented "faultless before the presence of His glory with exceeding joy." But in the courts of the heavenly city, through the cycles of eternity, there shall be a perpetual remembrance of all Christ taught and of all Christ wrought in the work of redemption. This is the burden of "the song of Moses, the servant of God, and the song of the Lamb." And yonder, we may imagine, more than here, where earth's clamorous noises so often drown the still small voice, will this mission of the Spirit be blessedly exercised. Here and there we shall know the presence of the Spirit and shall remember the gracious words of love divine.

# VI.

## HIGHER CRITICISM AND HUMAN DOCUMENTS.

*"Ye are our epistle, written in our hearts, known and read of all men; being made manifest that ye are an epistle of Christ, ministered by us, written not with ink, but with the Spirit of the living God; not in tables of stone, but in tables that are hearts of flesh."*—2 Cor. iii, 2, 3.

ONE of the signs of our times is the interrogation mark. It is a symbol of one of the fundamental characteristics of the Protestant Reformation. That mighty movement was made possible by the historical spirit. It began with an appeal from the ecclesiastical Cæsar to the historical Christ. The return to the Christianity of Christ was only possible by means of the record in the early Christian literature. Luther heard the voice of Christ in the Scriptures, and wherein he saw that Christ and Rome did not agree he was ready to follow Christ.

The attempt to realize the original idea of Christianity led to the recovery of the primitive literature of the Bible. There was found salvation by grace and the primary principle of the Reformation became justification by faith. Some things were missing in the record, such as penances, indulgences, and pilgrimages, and a more or less successful effort was made to discard them.

The seat of authority in religion was shifted from the Church to the Bible; the Bible was put into the hands of the people, and the right to read and interpret was claimed for all men. As a logical sequence of justification by faith came the right of private judgment in religion. That meant the revival of religious liberty, usurped by the Roman hierarchy and lost to the Christian world for centuries. This fruit of the Reformation has been slowly ripening for four hundred years. During that time the human mind has been free, but it has only gradually entered upon its heritage of liberty. With the knowledge of privilege there has developed the feeling of responsibility. Not only in religion, but in all departments of thought, the historical spirit has become pre-eminent. Everywhere there has been the impulse of original investigation. Nothing has been taken for granted. Popery in art, science, philosophy, and literature, as well as in religion, has been at a discount.

This historical spirit, limited in its mission at the beginning to the discovery of the meaning and immediate use of the original Christian documents, has enlarged the borders of its activities. It characterized the work of scholarship in all its investigations during the nineteenth century. Having received such impulse by its place in the dominant religious movement of the last four centuries; having subjected to the most rigid scrutiny the materials and sources of secular history; and having played havoc with the traditions of classic literature, it was to be expected that it would return to a re-examination of the historical literature of the Christian religion. The student of history can not ignore the Bible, and the lover of literature will linger among its treasures. And since revelation has been made in history, and the record is preserved in literature, the Bible has become the subject of study under the changed conditions. The result is what we know as "the higher criticism," regarded by some as a demon of destruction and by others as a guardian angel of truth.

The terms "lower criticism" and "higher criticism" describe the methods used by the new histor-

ical spirit in the investigation of all ancient literature. They are not exclusively the technical terms
of the modern phases of Bible study. The "lower
criticism" deals with the text of a document; the
"higher criticism," after the determination of the
text, gives us the historical interpretation. Whether
a certain reading in the drama of "Hamlet" is correct, is a question of the "lower criticism," and is
settled by appeal to such sources as the first folio
or the second quarto; but the debate as to whether
Shakespeare or Bacon wrote "Hamlet" belongs to
the province of the "higher criticism." The term
"higher criticism" is purely technical. In the lay
mind it is likely to generate a double prejudice.
Criticism, in common usage, is synonymous with
faultfinding and picking to pieces. The adjective
"higher" lacks felicity for the reason that it suggests the presumption of superiority. But, tech-
nically, criticism is a method of knowledge. A
critic is a *krites,* or judge. A criticism is an opinion. Having opinions and expressing them we are
all critics in ordinary. Criticism in literature stands
for careful, patient examination. The use of the adjective "higher" is purely incidental. It grew out of
the fact that the preparatory work of arranging a
pure text (rejecting interpolations, supplying omis-

sions, and adjusting transpositions), is called the "lower," because preparatory, criticism. But when the imperfections of the text, common in ancient manuscripts, because of the carelessness of copyists and other causes, have been eliminated as far as possible from the document, then the "higher" task of the critics is imposed.

Bible students are under a heavy debt of obligation to the "lower" critics. The scholars of Germany and England, who have devoted their energies to the justification of the text, are unknown to the majority of the devotional readers of the Scriptures. Much of their work to date, however, has been given to the public in the Revised Version. The "higher criticism," in contrast, studies the Bible as a great literature covering centuries of time. It applies the accepted principles and canons of historical research to the various documents. It deals with problems of date, authorship, integrity, literary form, and credibility. It asks concerning a document: Who was the author? When was it written? What were the circumstances of its production? Is it preserved in its integrity? If there have been changes, can it be restored to its original form? Is it trustworthy in statement? Is it confirmed or discredited by other sources of information? Is it prose or poetry, and what is its literary form under this general classification? These and similar questions belong to the "higher criticism."

It is apparent that in the field it covers it is very much a new name for an old thing. These questions have always been discussed by the Christian apologists, and specifically dealt with, in more recent times, by the authors of "Biblical Introduction." The difference is not in the ground covered by the "higher criticism" as much as it is a difference in spirit and method. It is also apparent that the "higher criticism" is to be regarded as an instrument of historical investigation, and not as a definite body of ascertained results. The term is frequently used as if it represented an aggregate of material antagonistic to the Christian religion. The fact is that its theories are tentative, and the spirit of order has not yet reduced its chaos. It should also be borne in mind that the value of any instrument depends upon the user. The Apostle Paul said that law was good if used lawfully. The maxim is of universal application. It is equally true of an ax or of the "higher criticism." The ax can be used for clearing a field or building a church; or it can be made instrumental in the destroying of a shrine or in the murdering of a man. Thus, too, with the historical method of interpreting the Bible. The use depends upon the user. If a scholar comes to the study of the Scriptures with invincible unbelief in the supernatural; with settled conviction as to the impossibility of miracle; with a fixed determination that everything in the records shall be accounted for by natural causes; his attitude is not only unscientific, but his work is sure to be destructive. Thus we have destructive and constructive workers in "higher criticism," and the whole movement bears the odium attaching to the work of the former.

What shall be our attitude? We can not escape the fact that a portion of divine revelation has come to us in the form of ancient documents. The Bible is an historical literature, and if we gain a genuine knowledge of it we must study it as literature. In this study the Bible asks fairness and not favors. The intelligent believer in the Book will not demand that it be exempted from the rules of evidence applied to other books. Objection to the closest scrutiny of the genuineness of the records is an evidence of skepticism and not a token of faith. Critical inquiry has full rights in applying the same tests of authenticity and credibility to the Scriptures that are used in dealing with other literatures.

Biblical investigation may be inspired by what has been called "the demon of criticism;" it may be carried on by those who are hopelessly committed to hostile preconceptions; it may misapply fair principles and refuse value to essential facts; and it may exhibit such a fanaticism of unbelief and such iconoclasm of purpose as to make the term a stench in the nostrils of sober scholarship. Even so, we have no authority to forbid trespassers. But we have defenders of faith, scholars of unquestioned ability, who know how to dispose of wood, hay, and stubble. There has never yet been an attack upon the Scriptures that has not reacted in augmenting their authority. While the battle of the giants continues there are only two things possible for Christian people—they must be on guard against error; and they must be ready to welcome the truth wherever it presents its credentials. The triumph of truth is the most comforting promise of God and the most assuring lesson of history. In all the centuries past the enemy has never captured an essential position or overthrown a vital doctrine. In the meantime there must be fair play, and those who, by reason of scholarly qualification and Christian experience, represent us in the conflict are entitled to sympathy and encouragement.

At present the existing results seem to demand a suspension of judgment. As an enthusiastic disciple of the school of "higher criticism" recently wrote: "To the scholars that have been over the ground nothing is so certain as that there is much that is uncertain." The critics are not agreed among themselves. Our attitude of fairness and our readiness to welcome truth do not mean that we are prepared to adopt half-baked theories or to swallow blood-raw conclusions that are the offspring of indecent haste. If we are not entitled to consign "higher criticism" to the limbo of disrepute because of the extraordinary differences in conclusions, when men are supposedly using the same critical principles, we certainly can not be asked to accept divergent results. Noticing the disagreements of the "higher critics," we can not help sympathizing somewhat with the strictures of Andrew Lang at the time of the publication of the Polychrome Bible. Speaking of the "polychrome" opinions of the critics, he wrote in an English review: "No color-box would contain pigments enough to print the contending opinions of the critics withal, if one offered a polychrome manual of criticism." But any satisfaction, born of such confusion of opinion among the critics, must be tempered by appreciation of

9

the fact that there is nothing approaching identity of belief on all subjects among Christians anywhere. Godly men are still praying for the unity of the faith. It remains to possess our souls in patience until that which the "higher criticism" holds in solution is precipitated, with an abiding faith that the final deposit will be wholesome. The process of elimination is continually going on, and is sure to leave a residuum of values.

Pending the outcome of critical dialectics in dealing with the ancient documents, what remains for those who do not possess the necessary apparatus for such work? The questions debated by the doctors are beyond the reach of individual investigation for the great majority. Only a few have the time, the training, and the tools for such labors; only a few have access to the convents and old-world libraries where the manuscripts are preserved; only a few can master the necessary sciences and languages and acquire facility in deciphering ancient documents; only a few can gain a first-hand knowledge of the disputed questions of probable authorship, original materials, and post-editing; only a few can distinguish the products of various periods finally gathered into the hymn-book of the Jewish synagogue; only a few are qualified to discuss the chronological arrangement of the materials in the Book of Isaiah. Where independent investigation is impossible intelligence on these and similar questions must wait on the toil of the specialists. "And God hath set some in the Church" who are teachers.

In the interval those who do not possess the special critical apparatus have a literature of revelation that can be "known and read of all men." For Christianity is not exclusively a book-religion. The Bible, of such priceless value in giving us the historical Christ and God's ways of revealing Himself in the past, is only one method of revelation. The primary unveiling of spiritual truth has never been given to man on paper. The characteristic method of God is to make Himself known in life and history. This is the highest revelation, and its study is the highest criticism. As expressed by some one, we not only have "Thus saith the Lord," but we also have "Thus doth the Lord." There are Gospels of Christ in personal experience. There are Acts of the Apostles wherever men live and work in the power of the Spirit. There are "living epistles" of the twentieth century as well as Epistles of Paul of the first century. There is an Apocalypse of the Christian centuries as well as the vision

of John on the Isle of Patmos. In a word, there
are human documents known to us all and continually open before our eyes. Their language of
speech, character, and conduct, all can read. The
Bible in flesh and blood challenges our attention and
demands our interpretation. Leaving the higher
critic, then, to, his chosen task of deciding dates,
identifying authors, classifying materials, testing
consistencies, and tracing relationships in connection with written documents, we turn our attention
to the more fundamental subject suggested by the
text.

We find our starting point in the acknowledged
fact that back of all literature, whether sacred or
profane, there lies life. Life is the only soil producing this growth. Literature is always and everywhere the expression of life. Back of history lie
the nations; back of biography is found the man;
back of poetry dreams the poet; and back of
prophecy is the prophet listening to the voice of
God. Homer, the father of literature (we use the
name and title only by courtesy of the critics),
found the materials of his great epics in Greek life
and tradition. A poem like the Iliad is a growth.
The ground work of the Homeric poems was still
earlier poems, which failed to survive. The songs

of the people, born of the universal experiences of love, joy, grief, and war, contributed their riches to form these literary treasures. The poems themselves are clear and animated pictures of early Greek life. Carlyle recognized the priority of life to literature when he described Dante as "the voice of ten silent centuries." The "Divine Comedy" was the joint product of the Florentine genius and the developing life of the thousand voiceless years. Into those centuries had been thrown the leaven of Christian doctrine and character, and by their transforming power the old civilization was passing away and a new order was taking its place. The new thought and life of Europe sought expression. Dante became its mouthpiece and gave to the world a revelation of that life in epic form. Shakespeare also exemplifies this truth. Not only was he identified with his time and his country,

"This blessed plot, this earth, this realm, this England,"

But by what has been aptly called "royal seizure," he confiscated the raw material for his work. Not only in historical plays did he gather from life, but now that all the plots of his dramas, with one exception, have been traced to their sources, we discover that he placed the world under tribute;

he "borrowed from humanity." The drama, Shakespeare's medium, has this in common with the epic—it describes life in action. Before we could produce anything worthy to be dignified by the name of American literature, we had to have more than a century and a half of American life. There are whole regions of the earth from which we expect nothing in letters for the simple and sufficient reason that in those parts no rich, strong life is seeking utterance. The vast majority of individuals have no contribution to make to literature because of their poverty of life. In men, and nations, and epochs, literature is the outcome of life.

All this is pre-eminently true of religious literature. The Bible is the autograph of life.. There was first the Hebrew people, and then followed the Old Testament writings. If these writings hold a place unique and supreme in the kingdom of letters, it is because they are the expression of a life without parallel in the annals of the race. This is apparent, of course, in the historical portions, where we read the narratives of the calling of Abraham, the fortunes of Joseph, the bondage in Egypt, the wilderness experience, the settlement of Canaan, and subsequent national vicissitudes. But it is also true that the higher literary forms of the ancient Scriptures, such as poetry and prophecy, are the efflorescence of a religious life. Such utterances were born of a divine inspiration in the human soul. The old Hebrew hymn-book, the Psalter, is a deposit of religious experience. It is the fruit of life. Its poetry is vital. Its pages reproduce the sorrows, the confessions, the fears, the doubts, the anxieties, the aspirations, and the thanksgivings of men. Experience inspired the utterance of the "Shepherd Psalm" with its abandon of trust: "The Lord is my Shepherd; I shall not want." Personal acquaintance with sin makes known its bitterness in the Penitential Psalms. Out of the abundance of the heart some mouth declared the consciousness of guilt and breathed a longing for forgiveness. There was precious personal knowledge back of the grateful utterance: "Blessed is the man whose transgression is taken away, whose sin is covered." We are confident that the declaration, "God is our refuge and strength, a very present help in trouble," was the overflow of a grateful heart in some hour of deliverance. This is a book of life—a life surcharged with exalted religious forces. The lyric poets of Greece and Rome gave the world nothing

like the Hebrew Psalms, for the good reason that
these people were strangers to such religious thought
and life as that of Israel.

The New Testament literature is likewise the
product of life. It is a group of books springing
up around the central figure of Christ. It is a revelation because it presents the person of Christ and
sets forth the significance of His appearance in history. "In Him was life, and the life was the light
of man." All its various portions must be read in
the light of His life and mission. If the New Testament is unique among books and striking in its sin-
gularity, the secret is found in the life it enshrines.
Out of the visible life of Christ came the Four Gospels in which, as suggested by Rothe, we of to-day
see "the historical Christ mirrored directly upon
the consciousness of those who surrounded him."
Out of the invisible life of Christ came what we
call the Acts of the Apostles—the acts of living
men inspired by a living Christ. The later didactic elements, found in the Epistles, follow after life
and history, to explain the life and to elucidate the
history.

The living Christ was at first the material and
vehicle of the revelation. He wrote no book. "The

life was the light of men." That revelation was first sent into the world in human documents. Between the life of Christ and the life of the world there was the mediating life of His disciples. The Christian life preceded the Christian documents. The truths were lived before they were written. The revelation of God's love was first made in the souls of living men and later was reduced to writing. Like our blessed Lord, the written documents are divine-human. Thus back of the first Gospel there are both the life of Christ and the life of Matthew, and hence we have the Gospel of Christ according to Matthew. There are the human voice and the divine inspiration. The truth is divine, and the experience and expression are human. "The life was the light of men." Jesus lived and died; rose from the tomb and ascended into heaven; the Holy Spirit was poured out upon His waiting disciples; the Gospel of salvation was preached; men believed on Him for the remission of sins; and the Church was organized and started on its career of conquest before Christianity possessed a single written document. The inspiration of living men was the initial task. In our religion life precedes literature.

This recital of facts is of special interest and of

vital importance as related to the "higher criticism" and its task. If the "higher critics" ever finish their work; if disputed questions of Bible dates, authorship, integrity, and credibility are all finally settled; the impregnable fact will remain that the literature, wherever written and by whomsoever written, was the product of life, and the living, producing cause must be taken into account. Life can not be annihilated by a critical theory. The history of the past can not be changed; it can only be studied and interpreted. Behind everything with which the new critical methods have to do is the life. That is not subject to Jehoiakim's penknife. Living men are back of all the documents, and if you throw the writings on the rubbish heap, those living figures of the past confront you and inquire as to what disposition you will make of them. The analogy holds in other sciences. Back of astronomy are the heavenly bodies, and without any particular reference to scientific theories—Ptolemaic, Copernican, or what not—the stars still swing and shine. Back of botany is the flora of earth, and without reference to the teaching of the naturalist the flowers themselves bloom in beauty and freight the air with perfume. Back of geology is the globe on which we live, and whatever may be the translation of its hieroglyphics by the scientists, its surface will afford solid ground for our feet and its harvest will fill our hungry mouths. Though all these sciences should be wiped out of existence, the realities upon which they are founded would remain; stars, flowers, and rocks would abide. Thus, too, the life out of which the written documents sprang is not subject to destructive critical theories, neither indeed can be.

The review thus far has been in the nature of a round of the outposts protecting the position of vital Christianity. Within these outer lines of defense are other and yet stronger entrenchments. For not only did the documents of the New Testament emerge from life and history; not only are that life and history indestructible by criticism; but, above and beyond all this, is the further fact that there has been, and is, a continued and increasing reproduction of the original sources out of which the Christian literature first sprang. This is the content of Paul's words in our text: "Ye are an epistle of Christ, ministered by us, written not with ink, but with the Spirit of the living God; not in tables of stone, but in tables that are hearts of flesh." The

canon of the written documents is closed, but the
human documents are being perpetually issued.
Each new-born Christian, rejoicing in God's mercy
and walking in white, is a living manuscript of revelation, carrying in his heart and life a Gospel that
may never know the written or printed form. Each
disciple of Christ is a volume, and a great host
that no man can number makes up the whole of the
Christian literature. The experience of each saint,
written or unwritten, is a life epistle expounding
the grace of God. He is an encyclical letter written
by the Holy Spirit. The message is so legible that
it can be "known and read of all men." This is
the religious literature first read by the world. For
this reason Christ could say of His disciples: "Ye
are the light of the world." The issuance of these
human documents, these "living epistles," will never
cease until the ancient prophecy is wholly fulfilled:

> "I will put My laws into their mind,
> And on their heart also will I write them:
> And I will be to them a God,
> And they shall be to Me a people:
> And they shall not teach every man his fellow-citizen,
> And every man his brother, saying, Know the Lord:
> For all shall know Me,
> From the least to the greatest of them."

We are told, in the defense of "higher criticism," that criticism is a method of knowledge, and wherever there is anything to be known the critical method has its place." We are informed that it is "the test of the certainty of knowledge, the method of its verification." Such being the nature and function of criticism, there is no reason why this method of knowledge may not be used in our study of human documents. We may put the same questions to "the living epistles" that the scholar asks concerning the primitive written documents. Take the problem of authorship for example. Suppose it is strictly true, as has been urged, that "there is not a single sentence in the Bible which lends a shadow of support to the orthodox doctrine of inspiration." Suppose it to be true that the written documents nowhere assert a divine authorship. There is one point, then, where the human documents are more explicit than the written literature. The living epistles echo the words of the Apostle Paul: "By the grace of God I am what I am." They bear ready testimony that they were written, as our text says, "with the Spirit of the living God." The divine inspiration of the Book may be disbelieved, but how is any one to get rid of the human testimony without abolishing all known rules of evidence?

We have laid aside the work of the famous chronologist, Archbishop Usher. His dates have disappeared from the margin of the Revised Version. They had no rightful place in any version. The scholars of to-day can not agree upon a Biblical chronology. It is one of the great confusions of the critics. In regard to the question of dates the "higher criticism" of human documents has the advantage. Not that all the living epistles are dated. But many of them are, and those that are lacking in this respect can easily be placed in their historical period. The time and circumstances of the production of many of these human documents constitute as sweet and definite an experience as the conversion of Paul. Thus the common student, without the equipment of the specialist, can apply the principles of the "higher criticism" to this abundant literature. The questions of integrity, credibility, and agreement with other related human documents on essential facts, are all open to examination. Nor will the investigator fail to reach a satisfactory conclusion because of lack of material, which is one of the greatest obstacles in the way of the ancient history critic.

It is a conceit, sometimes of scholarship and always of unbelief, that the faith of the vast majority of Christians is unthinking and second-hand. This grows out of the mistaken notion that Christianity is a book-religion, pure and simple. Compared with this "higher criticism" of life, the results of historical research must be declared hopelessly inferior. The man who reads the record of the Spirit in his own life and in the lives of others, is not irrational in his methods. The man who reproduces conditions, such as repentance toward God and faith in the Lord Jesus Christ, and by so doing gets the results of peace and power as described in the textbook, has a first-hand knowledge. He is as scientific in his method as the professor in the chemical laboratory arranging materials for an experiment, and securing anticipated results. Those who have this personal experience of the vital spiritual processes, described and promised in the Book, can say: "Now we believe, not because of thy saying: for we have heard Him ourselves, and know that this is indeed the Christ, the Savior of the world." It was of those with such revelation in life that John wrote: "Ye need not that any man should teach you." The man who has read the Gospel of Christ according to his mother; the man who has studied "the living epistle" in the life and character of a godly father; the man who has witnessed the acts of modern apostles at home, has had a Christian literature in his own tongue. The human documents can be known and read of all men. These "living epistles" are original sources; their study is the highest criticism.

# VII.

## THE FAILURES OF CHRISTIANITY.

*"And He spake many things unto them in parables,
saying, Behold, a sower went forth to sow; and
when he sowed, some seeds fell by the wayside,
and the fowls came and devoured them up: some
fell upon stony places, where they had not much
earth; and forthwith they sprung up, because
they had no deepness of earth: And when the
sun was up, they were scorched; and because
they had no root, they withered away. And
some fell among thorns; and the thorns sprung
up, and choked them: but other fell into good
ground, and brought forth fruit, some a hundred-fold, some sixty-fold, some thirty-fold.
Who hath ears to hear, let him hear."*—Matt.
xiii, 3-9.

THE achievements of Christianity have been so
illustrious, both in character and extent, as to com-
pel acknowledgment. The historical critic, whatever his school of thought, must deal with the un-

paralleled phenomenon of its rise and progress. Its
works lie embedded in nineteen centuries of human
history, and that history contains the best record of
the race. The center of its operations is found in
the sphere of character. It begins its work with the
transformation of the individual. It has demon-
strated its power in changing bad men into good
men. These products have been "the light of the
world" and "the salt of the earth." They have been
the torch-bearers of moral progress and the preserv-
atives against moral decay. This living energy has
been the most potent factor in producing the conditions under which we live; conditions deserving the
eulogy of a free-thinking observer: "Christianity
is a beautiful civilization." From this source has
come the inspiration of the highest and noblest in
our art, literature, philanthropy, legislation, thought,
and life. At the beginning it flung its new-born
forces at the heart of heathenism, and since that
time it has been in constant conflict with the hideous
vices and the hoary evils of the social order. So
widely influential has Christianity been that the
famous words of Richter fall upon our ears as sober
truth: "Jesus is the purest among the mighty, the
mightiest among the pure, who, with his pierced
hand, has raised up empires from their foundations,

turned the stream of history from its old channel, and still continues to rule and guide the ages."

The skeptical critic, with his scorn of the supernatural, has essayed the stupendous task of accounting for these achievements by natural causes. Such was the attempt of Gibbon in his "Decline and Fall of the Roman Empire," which, to a large extent, had to be a study of the rise and triumph of the Christian religion. He suggested five causes: zeal, purged of Jewish narrowness; the doctrine of a future life of reward and punishment; the ascription of miraculous power to the early Church; the pure and austere morals of the early Christians; and the warm affections and admirable discipline of the young republic. But each of these causes is also an effect, and as an effect demands explanation. What produced the zeal, the marvelous powers, the high morality, and the splendid discipline of the nondescript material out of which the early Church was built? These specified causes are themselves achievements, and the problem of the naturalist remains unsolved. This is the perpetual challenge of history to those who deny the divinity of our faith. The Christian apologists, too, have not neglected the use of the same material. Open a volume on "Christian Evidences" and you will find at least a

chapter devoted to the subject. History is called
upon to make its contribution to the external proofs
of the divine origin of Christianity. The witness
of the centuries has strengthened faith in the Gospel
of Christ as the power of God unto salvation, and
has placed an almost insurmountable obstacle in the
way of honest unbelief.

But, rejoicing in the success of Christianity, we
are not permitted to forget that its failures are also
in evidence. Its defeats have been only less conspicuous than its victories. That which has been
accomplished only throws shortcomings into bolder
relief. Its representatives have not been consistent;
its institutions have not been perfect; its enterprises
have sometimes lagged and sometimes failed; its
program of salvation has not been carried out. For
eighteen centuries it has attempted the redemption
of society, and while, without question, it has blessed
humanity in countless ways, our civilization can
only be called Christian by courtesy. The world has
not been purged of its corruption; its vices have not
been vanquished; its evils have not been destroyed;
its abuses have not been dethroned; its people have
not been saved from their sins. Christianity has
failed in the individual. Multitudes, who have been
in contact with the Gospel for years, have success-

fully rejected its overtures and withstood its influences. There are territories that were once aflame with zeal in which to-day the Church of the living God is scarcely a memory. There are nations, once swayed by a living faith, which have so far departed from the Christian ideal that they are almost barren of the fruit of the Spirit. Over against the splendid successes of our religion must be placed its undeniable failures. And this is the question that springs to the lips of the one who traces the course of the Gospel down through the Christian centuries. If Christianity is divine—if it is the power of God unto salvation—why has it not been uniformly successful and thoroughly effective?

Seeking an answer, we turn to the Master and find that this phase of the fortune of His kingdom was anticipated and explained in His teachings. The occasion of the forecast was a critical time in His own ministry in Galilee. In that northern country He had been incessantly at work for a whole year. His hand of power had been busy with its healing touch and His voice of love had been unceasing in its utterances of grace and truth. Far and wide spread the news of His works, and from the houses where His name had become a household word the people in multitudes crowded about Him.

From surface indications Jesus appeared to have conquered the hearts of the Galileans, and the rising enthusiasm, like a tidal wave, might reasonably have been expected to roll southward, overwhelming all opposition, nor staying in its course until Jerusalem had owned and crowned its King. The time seemed ripe for a triumphal progress to the throne of the house of David.

But our Lord was under no such illusion. He knew what was in man. He realized that the Galilean enthusiasm had reached its high-water mark, and that the tide would soon begin to ebb. He was not deceived by crowds that would soon vanish, by an interest that was transient, by impressions that were ephemeral, by emotions that were effervescent, by declarations of love and loyalty that in a brief moment could be transformed into bitter and blasphemous denunciations. In a little time, instead of being the center of attraction for thousands, He would be followed by a handful of disciples; instead of being the idol of the populace, he would be a fugitive avoiding publicity. But His disciples, we may be sure, estimated the significance of the crowds by their numbers, being deceived by their eyes. For the purpose, therefore, of checking any undue elation of spirit, any unfounded expectations, any imposition of appearances, and for the further purpose of preparing them for the hour of disenchantment, when the epidemic of enthusiasm would spend its force, He sounded the needed note of warning. For the shock of such an experience as this the disciples needed preparation. So he taught them that, between our sanguine expectation and our actual realization as heralds of the kingdom, provision must always be made for a wide margin of failure.

The warning was given in what is called "the Parable of the Sower." It was springtime by the sea of Galilee, and the crowds of eager listeners thronged the Master as He stood upon the shore. To escape the crush He stepped into a fishing-boat, and from that unique pulpit addressed the congregation before Him. His introduction was the parable in which we find the explanation as to why the preaching of the Gospel is not invariably successful. Interpreters have been at great pains to reproduce the physical surroundings. Upon the hillside beyond the people were the fields, and we are allowed to imagine that in the distance a farmer strode along scattering his seed. But the local color adds little to the interest of the parable. The moral aspect of the situation is the principal thing. Before the

speaker stretched away the sea of faces. He was a
sower of seed, and his audience represented the field
in which for twelve months He had been working.
What would be the harvest? Would all those who
had listened to His preaching produce the sheaves
of golden grain? The answer is negative and ex-
planatory. And while the pending situation was
the immediate occasion of the instruction, the general principle it contained applies to all congregations in which, as a field, the seed of the Gospel
might be scattered. It is a perpetual explanation
of the cause of the failures that would attend the
preaching of the Word.

This announcement of prospective failure must
have been a surprise. Apart from experience a far
different result would be prophesied for such a message and such a messenger. Taught by the Old
Testament the disciples would expect immediate and
complete triumph. Their religious education would
predispose them to the belief that the kingdom
would come without the slightest reference to human desire or disinclination; that Messiah would
conquer in spite of man's opposition and in the absence of man's co-operation. But the fond imagination that the divine desire guaranteed salvation to
all men simply by the proclamation of the Gospel,

was effectually dispelled by the parable. The publication of the good news would be attended by a
variety of results, and some of the results must be
reckoned as failures. The history of preaching
through all centuries and among all peoples cor-
roborates the truth of our Lord's prediction, uttered
in the face of his own great congregation on the
plain of Gennesaret.

The fact of failures being recognized, and the
prophecy of failures being recalled, the rationale of
the failures is our next concern. Causes have been
suggested. Two widely differing explanations have
been offered. The first comes from those who belong to the opposition. They lay the blame at the
door of religion itself; they insist that the weakness
belongs to the seed. Those who proffer this solution are usually ready to express appreciation for
what Christianity has accomplished in the past.
They acknowledge that it was an essential factor in
one stage of social evolution. In the name of progress, however, they contend that the ancient landmarks must be left behind in the onward march
of the race, and that some new star is needed to
guide humanity's future steps. They argue that
Christianity has done its work, has exhausted its
vital forces, and is now impotent to grapple with

existing conditions. Old and decrepit, it should be
treated with reverence for its works' sake, but it can
have no commanding office in the further development of man. Just as the patriarchal phase of religion was succeeded by the Mosaic era; just as
Judaism was superseded by Christianity; just so,
they assert, some fresh form, some higher type,
must follow the religion of Christ. Ignoring the
fact that the world has never risen even to the level
of the Ten Commandments; ignoring the fact that no
nation has ever yet given practical application to the
principles of the Sermon on the Mount; ignoring
the fact that no single class of Christians has at-
tained "the measure of the stature of the fullness of
Christ;" ignoring the fact that the proposed suc-
cessor is not yet in sight, they suggest that the ancient faith be retired. In other words, to use the
figure of the parable, the cause of the failure lies
in the seed.

The other theory of failures comes from those
who set themselves for the defense of the Gospel.
According to this view the indictment is against the
ministry; the sower of the seed is the culprit.
Some sowers are accused of scattering the seeds of
noxious weeds of heresy rather than the truths of
the Gospel. Other preachers are faulty in method;

they do not clothe the truth in attractive form; they can not fix the attention of their hearers; they do not secure the equipment of the Holy Spirit. These and other specifications are commonly supposed to account for the non-productiveness of preaching. That there is, and has been, legitimate ground for such charges may be conceded as lamentably true. But an hypothesis must cover the facts in the case, and when it is attempted to account for the failures in the proclamation of the Gospel by charging it all to dereliction on the part of the ambassadors for Christ, the explanation will not cover the experience of our Lord. His hand scattered good seed. He was not lacking in method; "never man spake like this man." He was equipped, having the Spirit without measure. Yet he knew the bitterness of failure. Some would not listen, and the fires of enthusiasm kindled in many hearts by His message soon settled into the cold, gray ashes of unconcern. Without making any defense of unfaithful men in the ministry, we insist that a theory must take care of all the facts.

The tragedy of failures is otherwise accounted for in the parable. Our Lord finds the cause—not in the sower and not in the seed; not in the preacher and not in the truth; but in the quality of the soil,

in the condition of the hearer. This is the lesson of
the parable: the growth of the seed depends upon
the nature of the soil in which it is planted. The
stress of the story does not bear upon the skill of
the sower. Elsewhere great emphasis is laid upon
the character and preparation of the preacher. Nor
does the parable question the quality of the seed;
that is guaranteed by its source and by its returns
in good soil. Here the Master points to the hearts
of men and declares: The crop depends upon the
soil.

This is quickly seen to be a universal law. The
farmer knows that it is true and rigid. He under-
stands that the planting of the best seed, and the
use of the most improved seeder will not insure a
crop. When everything else is present in perfection
the soil will govern the result. Likewise the Christ
teaches that the condition of the hearer is the deter-
mining factor in proclaiming the good news of the
kingdom. The seed finds the soil but does not
create it. What a man gets from the Gospel depends upon what a man brings to the Gospel. The
Germans have embodied this central idea in the title
they give the parable: "The Four Kinds of Soil."

The parable of the soil deals with aspects of the
kingdom that are public and patent. Its truth can

be verified by observation and substantiated by history. Other parables, notably that of the Pearl of Great Price, and that of the Hid Treasure, must be interpreted by experience. As a prophecy the details describe the diverse classes of hearers that compose all congregations, and the diverse results that will everywhere attend the preaching of the word. The differences specified lie upon the very surface of human nature, describing as they do the varying degrees of receptivity possessed by those who hear. The *beaten path,* the *shallow soil,* the *thorny ground,* are each typical of a class of hearers. The scribes and Pharisees, with minds hard-trodden by tradition; the Galileans, with their shallow and shortlived applause; the tentative discipleship with its profession, "Lord, I will follow thee; but—;" and the loyal circle of noble spirits, following Christ without reserve,—these are the prototypes of those who constitute the field of humanity. And even among the good and honest hearts there are diversities of attainment; for some bring forth an hundred-fold, some sixty-fold, some thirty-fold.

At this point the parabolic instruction ends. The teaching is equivalent to a statement of fact. Conditions are described as they actually exist, and these, we are told, account for manifest results. The

teaching enters into no consideration of the process
by which these qualities of human nature are produced; but given these conditions (and they are
certainly common, whatever their cause) the result
will be failures. Warning has been given against
pushing inquiry beyond the fixed boundaries of the
parable. But this is not a possible terminus with a
forest of interrogation marks just before us. Whence
arise these differentiations, here represented as qualities of soil? Are these distinctions of nature or of
character? Is it true that the Gospel has no chance
except with those who are predisposed by nature to
receive it? If so, where lies the responsibility for
the fact that a proportion of the race is immune to
religious influence? The parable does not concern
itself with these and similar questions. Taking
hearts as they are, it prophesies their reception of
the Gospel. But as students of the whole Word we
are not subject to such limitation. It is our privilege to study Scripture in the light of Scripture.
Writing an exposition of the parable of the kingdom for the preacher's use in the study, we might
pause here, but, preaching to living men and women,
in whose minds these great questions clamor for
answer, we must give them consideration. The
problems suggested by the wide diversity of results,

so picturesquely set forth as attendant upon the
preaching of the Gospel, may be reduced to two.

The first is found in the question: Are these
differences in receptivity *natural* or *acquired?* The
importance of the result of such an inquiry is apparent in the fact that upon it hinges the doctrine of
human responsibility.  If the disabilities described
belong to nature, then men came from the hand of
the Creator in such fashion that the proclamation of
the good news is not simply a useless form but a
veritable mockery.  The parable has actually been
used as an argument for such a belief.  It has been
interpreted as if it taught predestination in its bald-
est and hardest form.  The conditions unfavorable
to the reception of the truth, according to this view,
are imposed and not acquired.  The incapacity in
the hearer is declared to be inherent.  If this view
be correct, there is no escaping the conclusion that
the impervious soil was trampled hard by divine
power; that the thorns, choking the springing grain,
were planted by the divine hand; that the shallow
soil was so arranged by divine purpose; while the
good and honest hearts are such by divine election.

The figures employed in the parable are not con-
clusive in solving the problem.  There are indications in our Lord's interpretation of His words that

the obstacles enumerated are not natural but acquired. The thorns, described in the explanation as
"the care of this world and the deceitfulness of
riches," are not birthrights. The pathways of earth,
in which the seed can find no lodgment, are certainly beaten hard by the feet of man himself. Lack
of attention is the "wayside" hearer's trouble. This
means, not incapacity, but false direction of attention. The man who can fasten his mind upon business and current events, has the ability to use that
same power with reference to truth and the affairs
of the kingdom of God. But while the figures do
not help us as to the shallow natures and the good
and honest hearts, they are covered by the Christian doctrine of human responsibility. This is one
of the atmospheric truths of the New Testament,
everywhere present and laying its pressure upon
each human soul. Equally to the purpose is our
Lord's declaration that men must receive the kingdom of heaven as little children. Among other
things, that must mean the necessity of laying aside
acquired ways of thought and action, and a return
to the simplicity and trustfulness of childhood. The
whole tenor of Gospel promise, invitation, and
warning indicates that the obstacles are not natural
defects but acquired indispositions, induced by neg-

lect of the means of grace and the crowding of the life, limited in its capacity, with the things of time and sense.

More importance, by far, attaches to the second question: Are these qualities of the soil—these conditions of the hearers—*permanent* or *subject to change?* This is the problem of vital moment. Whatever may be the cause of existing conditions, whether the varieties of soil represent natural or acquired incapacity, the chief interest centers in the possibility of change. If human nature can know no change for the better we have only a Gospel of despair. Here again the parable throws light on only a part of the difficulty—the good and honest hearts. Its illustration does not touch all points. It sets forth only one aspect of the phenomena of the spiritual life. It seems to assume that the characters of the various classes of hearers are fixed and incapable of change. In nature, we must admit, that, as far as present knowledge goes, some soils are hopelessly unproductive. The great mountain ranges, the hot and barren sands of the desert and the white and silent ice plains of the poles, are hopeless fields for the agriculturist.

But, reading Scripture in the light of Scripture, we dare allow no interpretation of the parable to pass unchallenged that ignores the idea of conversion—the great Christian doctrine of transformation. An ancient school of heretics (the Gnostics) did indeed divide men into two classes—one capable and the other incapable of the Christian life, but there is no such brutal fatalism to be found in the Scripture. For while it is true, and the thought is awful in its significance, that there is such a possibility as laying waste the very soil of human nature in which the seed of eternal life should take root, it is also blessedly true, not only in promise but in experience, that, even for those who have brought themselves into such evil condition, a recovery through the grace and power of God is possible. Hence the Gospel of hope is for all men. There is one element in the soil of human nature, not found in the soil of the earth—freedom of choice. The man who longs for the salvation of his soul and the fruit of the Spirit has assurance of attainment in the divine promise. Just as the process of irrigation has transformed the arid lands of the great West, and made them beautiful and fruitful, so it belongs to the impregnable facts even of modern history that the grace of God has reclaimed the most unpromising soil of human nature and produced a harvest of good visible to the naked eve of the skeptical observer—Charles Darwin's memoirs bearing witness.

In keeping with this central teaching of the Christ are the words in which He concludes the parable: "He that hath ears to hear, let him hear," and the exhortation that follows the record as given by Luke: "Take heed therefore how ye hear." In these words are gathered up the practical lesson of the instruction for His own and all succeeding congregations. *On attention hinges destiny*—this is the finding of modern psychology and the reiterated warning of the Gospel. The power of attention belongs to man, and the direction of attention is dependent on his will. Herein lies the basis for the doctrine of responsibility as related to the hearing of the Word. The conclusion of the whole matter is this: "Take heed how ye hear."

The fact that these qualities of soil which determine the reception of the message are acquired, and not native, gives us the lesson with which to end the study. The soil should be pre-empted in behalf of the truth of Christ before receptivity is reduced to dangerous degrees. The parable points us to the fact, so slowly recognized, that youth presents the most productive period in religious results of all man's threescore years and ten. That time of life, bounded by the age of twelve at one extreme and by the age of twenty-four at the other, is the richest harvest-field because freest from the care of this world, the deceitfulness of riches, and all the other developing conditions that interfere with attention to the message of the ambassador of Christ. Compared with other periods, this stretch of a dozen years is like the teeming prairies of the Mississippi Valley in contrast with the barren alkali deserts of Utah and Nevada. Within these years there lies almost a monopoly of religious opportunity. Beyond this period the chances against conversion to God are almost appalling. Revival gleaners may have a mission outside this field, thus fenced off by age, but the harvest-hands will find the golden grain springing up most abundantly within these limits.

Profoundly impressive in this connection are some late findings of science. Recently investigators of recognized standing began systematic study of the phenomena of the religious life. Before that time the region covered by that part of human experience was a dark continent unexplored. Now the subject is enlisting an increasing number of scholars. As yet only a few of the pioneers in the new field of research have made public the results of their investigations, but, meager and tentative as the published statements are, they are almost startling in their significance.     In religion, the "sphere of influence," to use a current political phrase, is shown to be the time between childhood and manhood.     Before reaching the age of twelve, we are told that the normal child is scarcely competent to make a life choice; and that after the individual passes the age of twenty-four his susceptibility to religious impressions is reduced to a minimum and becomes a vanishing quantity.     During that period, however, even the processes of physical nature are ready to co-operate with religious forces brought to bear upon the developing life.     The great choices are made during this time, and the large majority who choose the Christian way do it within the space of these comparatively few years.

This conclusion is reached by scientific methods. Tables are prepared and exhibited on the same general principle as the "Law of Mortality" under which our life insurance companies operate.     This "Law of Mortality" is deduced from death records and from the experience of companies during a long series of years.     In this way is determined what average proportion of persons who enter upon a certain period will die during that period, and, consequently, what proportion will survive.     The statistics embodying the results are called "Tables of Mortality." On these, one of the most important of which is known as the "American Experience Table," are based the calculations of insurance experts as to "the expectation of life." In like manner the scientists, as a result of their investigations of religious experience, have published what may be designated as "Tables of Immortality," upon which might almost be based "the expectation of eternal life." They have secured from a large number of Christian men the facts of their religious experience. This material is analyzed to insure accurate information. The data is not as extensive as that employed by life insurance experts. It covers less than two decades while the insurance tables are the growth of a century. The work has been done by volunteers and not by professionals, for love of knowledge and not for commercial gain. Of the results secured none possess more vital interest than that which has to do with religious receptivity—the subject of the parable of the soils. Taking such materials as could be found in the life history of 776 graduates of Drew Theological Seminary, 526 officers of the Young Men's Christian Association in the United States and Canada, 272 members of the Rock River Conference of the Methodist Episcopal Church, and 1,784 men at large, independent investigators found the average time of conversion to be between sixteen and seventeen years of age. With this result the observation of Christian workers is found to agree.

What is the lesson? Plant the soil of life before it becomes unproductive! To all sowers of the seed, in home and Church, revelation and science repeat in unison: "He that hath ears to hear, let him hear."

NOTE.—On the occasion when this sermon was preached inquiry revealed the fact that out of a congregation numbering over twelve hundred, only one person had been converted after the age of forty years. For the figures given above I am indebted to a valuable work by Professor George A. Coe, bearing the title "The Spiritual Life."

# VIII.

## THE CORRELATION OF SPIRITUAL FORCES.

*"And there are diversities of operations, but it is the same God which worketh all in all."*—I Cor. xii, 6.

IN the physical world there are two great factors, and, as far as we know, only two. One is the substance of which all bodies, living or not living, are composed. The other is that which produces, or tends to produce, the movement or rest of bodies; a cause of which motion and restraint are the effects; and a cause known to us only by its effects. The first of these factors we call matter; the second factor we know as force.

The brilliant era of physical science in which we live, is, in large measure, the product of two discoveries concerning these factors of force and matter. The first of these discoveries dates from the closing years of the eighteenth century. At that time experimental science established the fundamental principle of the indestructibility of matter. The acceptance of the theory was, of necessity, revolutionary in its results. The notion that matter could be destroyed was fatal to chemistry. The analysis of the chemist, who accounted for the disappearance of materials in his processes, by the simple theory of destruction, was comparatively worthless. But after the acceptance of the dogma of the indestructibility of matter, it became an axiom of the laboratory that not a single atom of matter could be destroyed. The new chemistry taught that while matter "changes form with protean facility, traversing a thousand cycles of change, vanishing and reappearing incessantly, yet it never wears out or lapses into nothing." The task of the chemist was now enormously increased, for he must render account for every thousandth part of a grain of the material with which he began his work.

The acceptance of this doctrine of the indestructibility of matter was followed and paralleled in the nineteenth century by a similar discovery concerning force. It is a principle of modern physics that no force is ever lost; that as matter appears in one form, and disappears only to survive in another form, so also does force. The law of the conservation of energy, as this great fundamental principle of modern physics is known, embodies the theory that no force is created or destroyed in any of the processes of nature, and that the total energy of the universe is constant. Coupled with this law of the conservation of energy is that of the correlation of forces. According to this scientific doctrine physical forces possess the property of convertibility. They are so intimately related that each may produce, or, in turn, pass into all the others.

The story of this theory of the correlation of forces belongs to the romance of science. More than one hundred years ago an American, Benjamin Thompson (later and better known as Count Rumford), made experiments respecting the relation of motion to heat. He found that the friction of two bodies always produced a certain amount of heat; and that the motion of a body, when arrested or hindered, likewise resulted in heat. For example, a portion of the heat generated in the locomotive on the modern railroad, is converted into the motion of the train; while, by the application of the brakes, or the friction of an axle, the motion of the train is transformed into the heat of friction. As a result of the experiments of Count Rumford, the scientists revised their creed as to the article on heat (up to that time generally considered to be a form of mat-

ter termed caloric or phlogiston), having reached
the conclusion that heat as it exists in bodies is a
form of motion.  With this as starting point the
theory of the correlation of forces was developed.

Count Rumford, in his experiments, showed that
heat, developed in boring a brass cannon for a couple
of hours, would raise nearly twenty pounds of water
from the freezing to the boiling point.  In the meantime the metal lost no weight, forcing the conclusion that heat could not be matter, but a kind of motion produced in the particles of matter.  Other experiments were offered in evidence.  Sir Humphrey
Davy found that by rubbing together two pieces of
ice, at a temperature below the freezing point, sufficient heat was produced to partially melt them.
Others called attention to the fact that to shake
water in a bottle raised its temperature.  But the
great demonstration was first made by Mr. Grove,
an English physicist, in 1843.  He invented and exhibited an apparatus by means of which, beginning
with a ray of light as an initial force, he obtained
a chemical action of electricity, of magnetism, of
heat, and of motion.  The schoolboy of to-day is
familiar with the fact that, beginning with the force
of electricity, we can obtain motion, or heat, or
light, or magnetism, or chemical affinity.  The mu-

tual relations of all these phenomena can be shown
equally well by taking mechanical motion as an
initial force. A block of marble hoisted by work-
men to the top of a building may be used. Suitable
apparatus will enable the experimenter to lower the
building block to the ground in such a way as to
secure heat, light, and electricity. The modern
science of physics rests upon the principles that all
energy is conserved, and that physical forces are
mutually convertible.

Beyond the purely scientific values of such discoveries, there lies their religious significance. In
the language of the universal creed, we believe in
"God the Father Almighty, Maker of heaven and
earth," and we must give a cordial welcome to that
which interprets the work of His hands. It is the
teaching of Scripture that all nature is intended to
be a perpetual witness to God's being, power, wisdom, and goodness. "For the invisible things of
Him since the creation of the world are clearly seen,
being perceived through the things that are made,
even His everlasting power and divinity." It was
a devout old reformer, before Luther's time, who
spoke of the Bible as "God's abridged revelation,"
in contrast with nature, the original and unabridged
message. There may be those among the scientists

who are willing to stop at nature, but there are others who, in the words of the late Professor John Fiske, push "through nature to God." The reverent study of "that universal and public manuscript," shows that each part bears the divine signature. The devoted heart presses nearer to the "Maker of heaven and earth" in each new scientific discovery. The man of faith rejoices in the increasing knowledge of the action of physical forces as disclosing more intimately the personal will of God.

Nearly three thousand years ago, with all the limitations of his time as to knowledge, a man of contemplative mind thus voiced his praise in appreciation of the world of nature: "O Lord, how manifold are Thy works! in wisdom hast Thou made them all: the earth is full of Thy riches." What would have been his wonder and exaltation had he lived in our own time of microscope, telescope, and spectroscope, when the horizons of knowledge are being continually pushed back; when the sphere of intelligent wonder is being so immensely enlarged; and when the glories and mysteries of the divine works are being indefinitely multiplied? For these times of investigation, in which men are so laboriously deciphering the hieroglyphics of nature, are giving an increasingly richer content to the utterance of the sweet singer of Israel:

> "The heavens are telling the glory of God;
> And the work of his hands doth the firmanent declare:
> Day unto day poureth forth speech;
> And night unto night revealeth knowledge."

And when we mark power at work in the universe; when we are taught that it works according to plan, and produces intelligible results; when we are justified in the hypothesis that all manifested power comes from a central source; when even Mr. Herbert Spencer speaks of "an infinite and eternal energy from which all things proceed," with reverent and grateful emotions we look out upon the realm of matter and force, and repeat the words of our text: "And there are diversities of operations, but it is the same God which worketh all in all."

Above the physical forces, with which we have thus intimately to do, we find other forces. The most superficial observer can not fail to see their operations in the world of human nature. The motive powers of human action offer themselves for rational consideration, as do the forces of the physical world. The reality of emotion is no more to be questioned than is the reality of motion, and it is as vitally related to our interests. The moving

power of affection is as real in social relations, as is
the use of steam in the industrial realm. The influence of mind upon mind, heart upon heart, and
will upon will, is as much a verity as the sway of
chemical affinity over material elements. The
storms that agitate the bosom of the sea no more
belong to the world of force than do the gusts of
passion and the blasts of anger that sweep through
human life. The influences that hold individuals
together in that great aggregate we call society, or
in the smaller group we know as the family, are as
truly forceful as is the mysterious power of gravity,
to which we ascribe the order and harmony of the
heavens. That which effectively and permanently
influences human life in any sphere must be a force,
and is entitled to be known and studied as a force.

Among the potent forces of the world are its
religions; and among the religions the most powerful is that called Christianity. It has not escaped
notice that this is the one religion that offers itself
as spiritual power. Socrates, in old Greece, standing among his fellows like some high mountain
catching the first glow of the coming sunrise of
truth, was a great moral teacher. He gave his disciples directions for the conduct of life, and specu-
lations as to the possibilities and destiny of man.

But having taught men what they ought to do, Socrates never ventured to promise, "Ye shall receive power." So the sage of China, practical Confucius, formulated his admirable code of ethics for coming generations, but the outcome depended on the unaided efforts of those who sat at his feet. He dared not close his instructions with the promise, "Ye shall receive power." The Buddha could give his counsels of perfection to those who joined his revolt against Brahmanism, and thus become "the Light of Asia." But Asia needed power as well as light, and Gautama's best was an unassisted program of culture for weak human nature. He taught his followers that victory must be their own; help from without, or above, was not to be expected. His religion was lacking in the inspiration of the promise, "Ye shall receive power." This is a fatal lack. A revelation of duty is but the lesser part of man's need. There may be mental receptivity as to lofty teaching, coupled with moral inability as to performance. Knowledge of the right is not sufficient. What we need, most of all, is an enabling act.

But the Christ, "who spake as never man spake," did something more and higher than to tell the blind that they ought to see, the deaf that they ought to hear, the dumb that they ought to speak, the degraded that they ought to rise, and the sinners that they ought to be good. He did not mock humanity by impossible visions of excellence. But of all teachers, He was the one who promised aid to willing souls that they might make the splendid ideals of His teaching shining realities in their living. His was the promise to discipleship: "Ye shall receive power." Force is promised in the manifesto of our religion. It suggests Christianity as a mighty power in individual life and human history. It sets the new religion forth as force, as energy, as spiritual motion. Its great apostle to the outlying nations could face imperial Rome, the mightiest fabric of government ever lifted to power and held in place by force of arms, with the declaration: "For I am not ashamed of the Gospel: for it is the power of God unto salvation." Wonderful promise of a wonderful Savior! In this higher life our need is great. Here our weakness presses us to the verge of despair. We need power to counteract the evil tendencies of our natures more than we need physical power to carry our crafts upstream against the currents, or across the sea against winds and tides. We need some power to lift us toward the heights of virtue, more than we need steam to carry us swiftly

12

over the plains, across the rivers, and through tunneled mountains. We need some power to help us perform the higher duties of life, more than we need mechanical devices whereby we can accomplish the work of one hundred men in a day. The machinery of human nature needs adequate motive power.

It need not be argued that Christianity has been and is, a definite force in the world. That would be a work of supererogation. It has been a more essential factor in the progress of humanity than steam-power or electricity. It has been active and aggressive, impetuous and imperious. The history of the world presents no phenomenon more striking than the manifested power of Christianity. It has produced a distinct epoch in history—the Christian era; it has introduced a new type of man by transformation, not Jew, not Roman, and not Greek, but a type so unlike existing types that it needed a fresh term to describe it, and the new name was given at Antioch; it has organized, and has maintained for almost two millenniums, the most catholic and powerful society the world has even seen—the Christian Church; it has created a civilization so unique in character, that it is described only by the adjective Christian. In its infancy it triumphed over the triple alliance of Jewish hate, Roman might and Greek

subtlety; it extirpated idolatry as it existed in that
ancient world, and from the Euphrates to the At-
lantic, and from the sluggish Nile to the forests of
Germany, the gods have vanished, while temples,
priests, altars, and worshipers have utterly passed
away. It is most powerful in those foremost nations
which have behind them a thousand years of development, and which seem to have a sustained monopoly of progress; it has inspired in the past century
missionary enterprises never equaled in history,
with results surpassing even those of the first century of Christian propagandism; it has created a
literature without a parallel at the expense of ages
of toil; it has founded and sustains Church build-
ings for worshipers, colleges and schools for students, hospitals for sick and disabled, homes for
aged and infirm, and asylums for orphans—a great
galaxy of beautiful philanthropies. All this and
more. Christianity has been, and is, a force in the
world. As such it demands, by its nature and
achievements, recognition and respect.

We can name the initial force out of which
spring all the diversities of operations that characterize our religion. We know the power by which
all the wonders of Christianity have been accomplished. The secret is revealed in one word—Love.

This is the keyword of our faith. It is the word most characteristic of the New Testament. It is the word most expressive of the nature of God and the spirit of Christ. Paul reaches the heights as he sings the psalm of its perfection and power, and John strikes it again and again like a chord of sweet music. It describes the source of salvation: "God so loved the world." It embodies the essence of Christianity: "Thou shalt love the Lord thy God;" and "Thou shalt love thy neighbor as thyself." It is the motive power of the new life: "The love of Christ constraineth us." It meets all the demands of the divine will: "Love is the fulfilling of the law." It is the proof of our profession: "By this shall all men know that ye are My disciples." Without this, all other gifts are of no avail. We may have eloquence ("the tongues of men and of angels"); we may have learning ("the gift of prophecy, and know all mysteries and all knowledge"); we may have faith ("all faith, so as to remove mountains"); we may have philanthropy ("if I bestow all my goods to feed the poor"); we may even make the supreme sacrifice of martyrdom ("and if I give my body to be burned"); but without love there is no Christianity. It is no more certain that the great forces that throb and pulsate in mechanics have their origin in heat, and that that in turn can be traced to its source in the sun, than it is that the dynamic of Christianity is love.

When love is thus designated as the essential force in Christian life and achievement, we face a problem of no mean proportions. Other qualities are set forth as requisites of symmetrical character. There are graces and virtues that must be reckoned as necessities in the new life. What of these? We have thought of love as the central figure of the personified Christian forces, but surrounded by a host of other fair forms. Perhaps we remember a picture, "The Three Graces," popular in former days, which gave us a vision of the sisters three who forever haunt the thirteenth chapter of First Corinthians. The picture disclosed three beautiful female forms in flowing robes. In the center of the group of three, with a suggestion of queenly, protecting strength, stood Love. Upon the bosom of Love, in trustful pose and happy content, rested the head of Faith; while encircled by the arm of Love, Hope stood looking, with expectant eye, into the far distance. The picture would further have suggested our thought of the forces of the Christian life, if there had stood in the background a great company, like a Greek chorus, each figure typical of some one

Christian grace or virtue. There would have been modest Humility, smiling Cheerfulness, open-handed Generosity, kindly Sympathy, chaste Purity, mild-eyed Gentleness, broad-shouldered Patience, winsome Courtesy, upright Integrity, and a host of others with which Christianity has peopled our thought. There are nearly as many of them as there are original elements in matter, or specific modes of motion in force. What of all these? The question is an intensely practical one, when we remember that each and all of these graces and virtues must have place in our lives, making the Christian personality a new Olympus, where heavenly divinities have their home. The aspect of Christian character thus presented is one of confusion. There is an absence of unity and simplicity in such a conception of the elements of character and the forces of life.

The problem becomes ever more personal and practical in the realization that we are cultivators of character; that the Christian ideal is perfection; and that symmetry demands that no one of these elements be lacking or dwarfed. In our efforts to this end, we have laid out character after the similitude of the old-fashioned garden-plot, with which the experiences of childhood made many of us familiar. You remember how there were spaces devoted to each kind of flower or vegetable—the peas here, the corn there, and the potatoes yonder. In such a way we seem at work cultivating our graces and virtues. We have love here, patience there, and humility yonder. We weed, dig, and water here, and then pass in our work to another part of our garden of character. But while we are busy cultivating one quality, the weeds seem to be choking others. This distressing lack of anything like unity and simplicity in our labor tends either to discourage us or to render us satisfied with small things.

This impediment has been recognized by many, and methods of relief have been proposed. The most notable attempt is probably that of the late Professor Henry Drummond, in his famous address, "The Greatest Thing in the World." In that address he treats Love as a compound, whose elements may be distinguished by analysis. In illustration of his thought, he likens Love to light. He says: "As you have seen a man of science take a beam of light and pass it through a crystal prism; as you have seen it come out on the other side of the prism broken up into its component parts—red, and blue, and yellow, and violet, and orange, and all the colors of the rainbow—so Paul passes this thing, Love, through the magnificent prism of his inspired intel-

lect, and it comes out on the other side broken up
into its elements." This Professor Drummond calls
"the Spectrum of Love, the analysis of Love." Of
course, we can not accept such teaching either as
psychology or theology. Love is not a compound
made up of a certain number of ingredients. It
can not be produced by mixing other elements in
due proportion. It is not to be compounded according to a prescription furnished by the Apostle Paul
or any one else. It is not a thing of shreds and
patches.

When the Master said that the law and the
prophets were found in the injunctions, "Thou
shalt love the Lord thy God," and "Thou shalt love
thy neighbor as thyself," He proclaimed the unity of
force in the religious life. When the great apostle
declared, "Love is the fulfillment of the law," he
stated the same principle in other words. Just as
the physical forces are forms or manifestations of
some one force, so are the forces of the Christian
world. Love is the promise and potency of each and
all the graces and virtues. Love has in it the latent
energies of all the motive powers of Christian activity. Love possesses such properties of convertibility that, by its multiplied modes of manifestation,
it can produce all graces and virtues. Each of these

—patience, benevolence, fidelity, courage, and all the others—can be reduced to some activity of Love. Just as the physical forces can be ideally reduced to forms of motion—as that we can say that sound is motion, light is motion, heat is motion—so each element of Christian character is a specific manifestation of Love. Thus Love, moving under various conditions, directed towards various objects, working towards various ends, discovers itself in various ways. We mark the specific manifestation, call it a Christian grace, and give it a distinguishing name. In other words, we have the correlation of spiritual forces, with Love as the initial force.

This theory of the correlation of spiritual forces is not a novelty, except in statement and illustration. Centuries before the scientists accepted the dogma of the persistence of force, the doctrine of the persistence of the supreme force of the Christian life was enunciated by the Apostle Paul in the words, "Love never faileth." And in that same chapter we have a statement of the doctrine of the convertibility of this initial force. "Love suffereth long"—then it becomes patience and resignation. "Love is kind"—then it becomes kindness and sympathy. "Love envieth not"—then it becomes good will and magnaminity. "Love vaunteth not itself, is not puffed up"—then it becomes modesty and humility. "Love doth not behave itself unseemly" —then it becomes civility and courtesy. "Love seeketh not her own"—then it becomes service and sacrifice. "Love is not easily provoked"—then it becomes forbearance and long suffering. "Love believeth all things"—then it becomes faith. "Love hopeth all things"—and hope is a method of Love's activity. Here in this marvelous exposition of Love's capacities are found the constituent elements of Christian character; all the graces that adorn the life of the individual; and all the forces that are operating to bless humanity and honor God. Any element not mentioned specifically will fall under some one of the sweeping generalizations.

Special notice is called to the fact that there is here no hint of love as a compound, produced by the bringing together of various ingredients. It is a description of the activities of Love; an apocalypse of the powers of Love; a declaration of the transformability of Love. Love does all these things that sweeten and brighten and bless humanity. Just as electricity heats, moves, lights, and heals, so Love endures, sympathizes, serves, sacrifices, is kind, benevolent, modest, and courteous. It is convertible into the various graces and virtues of the Chris-

tian character. This gives the religious life a unity
and order analogous to that of the physical world.

Here, then, is the open secret of the higher life;
it lies in a loving heart. Out of the heart in which
the love of God has been shed abroad, will be the
issues of life. We are told that science, following
a hint given by Young, now employs the terms energy, usually held to be synonymous with force, to
signify the power of doing work, in whatever that
power may consist. That quiet, latent ability for
doing something, such as lifting the hand or speaking a word, is called potential energy. We are
familiar with the potential energy of the great res-
ervoir of water, which is behind each little stream
pushed into our houses when we turn a faucet. We
can understand that when the old clock is wound
once a week, energy is stored up from the arm of
the one who performs the task, and the clock will
go on ticking and telling the time until that energy
is exhausted. We are interested in the suggestion
that if the capstone on one of the great pyramids
were lowered to the ground, the energy expended
by the forgotten slaves who lifted it to its place,
would be released. But we are more interested to
know that the human heart, charged with love, has
in it all the potential energies of Christian life and

history, and as condition after condition, circumstance after circumstance, contact after contact, duty after duty, call them forth, the result is a manifestation, known and named as a grace or virtue. And, remembering the Giver of the great gift, we can add: "And there are diversities of operations, but it is the same God that worketh all in all."